The African American Christian Parent: Parenting In The Context Of A Spiritual Deficit

Eddie B. Lane

Black Family Press Copyright 1997 Eddie B. Lane
The African American Christian Parent:
Parenting In The Context Of A Spiritual Deficit

Black Family Press Copyright 1997

All Rights Reserved.

No part of this publication may be reproduced, stored in a retrieval system electronically or mechanically, or transmitted in any form or by any means. Neither may it be photocopied, recorded or otherwise, except for brief quotations without prior written permission from the holder of copyright.

Publisher

Black Family Press
1810 Park Row
Dallas, Texas 75215
(214) 428-3761

Published in the United States of America

Cover Design: Fame Publishing Inc.

TABLE OF CONTENTS

Acknowledgements   vii

Foreword   ix

Introduction   xi

PART 1
PARENTING PRINCIPLES FROM THE BOOK OF PROVERBS

Chapter 1
Spiritual Bankruptcy   3

Chapter 2
The Priority: Spirituality   16

Chapter 3
The Key: Skillful Living   26

Chapter 4
Train Up a Child: Preaching to the Wind   30

PART 2
TELLING IT LIKE IT IS

Chapter 5
Problems Faced by African American Parents   43

Chapter 6
Raising a Child in a Violent Society   50

Chapter 7
Educating a Child in a Racist Society   61

TABLE OF CONTENTS

Chapter 8
Double Consciousness: An African American Reality   71

Chapter 9
Black Nationalism and Acculturation   76

PART 3

ROLES AND RELATIONSHIPS IN PARENTING AFRICAN AMERICAN CHILDREN

Chapter 10
The Role of the African American Father   85

Chapter 11
The Role of the African American Mother   93

Chapter 12
The Role of the African American Church   97

Chapter 13
The Role of African American Children   100

Chapter 14
The Role of Parenting in Formal Education   110

Chapter 15
The Role of the Extended Family   114

Chapter 16
The Role of the Community   117

PART 4

PREPARING FOR PARENTHOOD

Chapter 17
Understanding the Basic Needs of Children   121

Chapter 18
Parenting from the Back of a Hearse   136

TABLE OF CONTENTS

PART 5

THE PARENTING PROCESS

Chapter 19
Preparing the Nest — 143

Chapter 20
Conception and Birth of the First Child — 148

Chapter 21
Building an Adult — 151

Chapter 22
Managing the Development Process — 164

Chapter 23
Managing the Education of the Child — 170

Chapter 24
The Completed Product — 181

PART 6

WHERE DO WE GO FROM HERE?

Chapter 25
Parenting in the 21st Century — 189

Conclusion — 198

ACKNOWLEDGMENTS

Both my wife Betty and I were blessed to have been born to exceptionally good parents. They raised children who had a love for the Lord and a taste for that which is good, in spite of living in a depressed community in an oppressive society.

Betty was fortunate to have had the opportunity to grow up with a strong extended family. She had two living great-grandmothers, two living grandmothers, and a host of aunts and uncles who participated in her formative development. Her most positive memories are of the quality time spent with her grandfather. Precious are her recollections of excursions with him.

Her mother, my dear mother-in-law, is a remarkable woman. Materially, she provided my wife with the best that she could which was quite an accomplishment in and of itself. However, the most important thing she gave my wife was a strong sense of pride and integrity. My wife is a refection of the quality woman that her mother is.

My parents were both committed to the idea that their children would become significant outside of the community in which they were raised. To this end they prioritized education, clean living, and hard work. Although my father was functionally illiterate, he still made sure that I not only went to school but that I graduated. I shall never forget the look on his face when I preached my first sermon. Witnessing my graduation was the fulfillment of a dream and hearing me preach was akin to delightful amazement.

My father was a strong man who spoke his mind and stood up to people when he felt they were wrong. He was a man of integrity and he had a sense of self worth that he expressed in what he wore, the car he drove, and the food he ate. My mother was a woman of quality who taught me how to love people. I was always her baby and she was ever my primary cheerleader. It was my privilege to have pastored my mother until she went to be with the Lord.

My dad taught me strength and fortitude. My mom taught me how to forgive. They both taught me how to love. Betty and I dedicate this book to our parents. May God use it to His glory.

I must also thank the number of people who so graciously gave of their time and money to the production of this book. These people include Mary Helen Crossland, Don and Charalett Test, Lin Williams, and the membership of Bibleway Church.

FOREWORD

You may well be thinking, why another book on parenting? To some extent you are probably correct. However, this book has the distinction of being specifically contextualized to parenting African American children from a bibliocentric and Christocentric perspective.

The parenting principles set forth in this book are both bibliocentric and Christocentric. Thus they are applicable to parenting in any racial or cultural context. However, this book is titled, *The African American Christian Parent: Parenting In The Context Of A Spiritual Deficit*. This title is designed to call attention to the idea that for African Americans, parenting has a distinct social, economic, political, and spiritual context that requires the contextualization of biblical principles to the African American parenting situation.

The context in which the African American parents has a unique history whose legacies remain until this day. One such legacy is that of slavery. The other is the African American church. In African American history there has been no other experience that has had such a profound and lasting impact on black and white Americans as has the institution of slavery. I think American black and white race relations today were shaped by slavery. The mold that shaped race relations in the postslave era was the legalized slave codes in the form of Jim Crow laws. Legalized segregation was designed to separate races. It gave birth to segregated housing, schools, and continued the tradition of segregated churches.

Inherent in segregation along with the idea of separate but equal was the notion that whites were superior to blacks. Most damaging of all was the idea propagated by whites that black people were an inferior race—a race of people fit only for manual labor. It is this legacy that must be addressed with both Christocentric and bibliocentric parenting principles. Nothing else works.

Slavery, in spite of its horrors, was the context in which black people developed a culture that was uniquely their own. It is a mixture of influences from Africa—immigrants from every land that came to these shores and the indigenous groups who settled this land.

I realize that some may find the title and focus of this book somewhat distasteful. However, it seems fair to me to use my biblical, exegetical, and expositional skills to extract and apply the word of God to that racial, social, and cultural context that I know best.

The second legacy that led to my decision to focus on the African American Christian parent is the legacy of the African American church in the African American community. Since the founding of the first black church in 1777, African American religion has become the focus of most of the significant activities in the black community.

This religious activity has given rise to the idea that in the African American community Christianity is the prevailing lifestyle. It is the thinking of no small number of black people that the church can combine the sacred and the social with no difficulty. In reality, however, the black church is hardly considered as an institution with a message for black people in the twenty-first century.

There is a serious spiritual deficit in the African American community today. The primary cause of this spiritual deficit is the existence of a weak church. The weakness of the black church is evident in its failure to reach black men and its failure to reach black youth.

It often seems as if the social and political heritage of the black church is considered to be that which makes it relevant today. What happened to the spiritual component? In my view the failure of the African American church has significantly contributed to the failure of the black family in both the middle class and the poor black communities.

Introduction

Most North Americans define parenting as a process involving the care and rearing of children within a nuclear family of a husband, his wife, and their children living together in the same household. This recognizes the father as the provider, protector, and authority in the home. In this structure, the mother is a homemaker whose primary responsibility is keeping the home and tending the children. This is the biblical ideal of parenting.

The traditional American models of this definition of parenting were reflected in the past in such television shows as "The Donna Reed Show," "Ozzie and Harriet," and "Leave it to Beaver." These shows, though legendary in their depiction of the supposedly typical white American family, can hardly be said to have defined either the African American family as it existed in the past nor does it define parenting for the modern day African American parent.

In a real sense parenting North American style has always meant being white by birth or at least by acculturation. It meant embracing a value system and lifestyle that reflected white values regardless of their relevance to the African American world and its complex forms of family.

To look back at the history of parenting in the African American community is to be reminded of a horrific history. It is to remember the fact that for more than two hundred years in the United States there was no such thing as an African American family with legal standing in a court of law. The idea of parenting was not a part of the recognized black experience. The black community was in fact not respected by whites as a community of families.

The United States legal system did not recognize marriage among slaves. In order to marry, slaves jumped a broom in a yard without legal or religious recognition of the marriage. Thus children born to slaves did not belong to the man and woman who bore them; they belonged to the slave master who owned the mother and father of the children. Even when the slave master acknowledged the mother of the children, he would deny the father any recognized authority in the lives of the children.

It is well to be reminded here that even in this horrid context of human existence the idea of family and parenting was alive and well among slaves. Many authors have sufficiently documented the fact that even in slavery some black families were able to maintain some semblance of a family unit. In addition, when slavery ended many slaves searched diligently to find their family members. To avoid marrying into their own family blood line many former slaves opted to marry Native Americans.

After slavery was abolished, the slave codes were reinstated in the form of Jim Crow laws in the South and defacto segregation was the order of the day in the North. Racial segregation by its very nature made it impossible for black men to be viewed as fathers according to the traditional American definition. They could not see themselves as fathers. How could they provide, protect, and lead their families while the wives remained home? In many households the wife was often more secure in her employment than was her spouse. Few African American children had the privilege of growing up in an environment where their father was recognized by the public as the authority figure in the home. Those who did were those who had assimilated, and thus closely resembled the white family structure.

The African American family in the postslave era was a family in search of structure, security, and identify. It was a family in search of a value system and a lifestyle that fit with the black American experience. This structure for most African Americans was not to be found in the family model of the white community.

In the African American home of the postslave era the parenting process was not dominated by the mother as myth portrays. The African American male emerges in this era as the authority figure in a home in which his children often felt more fear than love. While short on the

INTRODUCTION

expression of love for his family, he was strong on authority.

As was the case with most of my generation, I grew up in a family where my mother had an eighth grade education which might have been equivalent to a high school diploma today. My father, on the other hand, was functionally illiterate. He could neither spell nor write his name and yet he was the authority in our family.

The definition of family in the African American community was never limited to the nuclear family. Although such households were the norm in the African American community, the definition of family was more complex. Any combination of relatives (blood and adopted) was possible. It may have consisted of a household with two sisters and their brother, an older woman with her unmarried daughter and her grandchildren, etc.

In defining family the African American experience historically demands that the term "family" be broad enough to encompass the whole of the community. It is not fitting to accept the Eurocentric concept of family as the standard for defining and evaluating the African American family. The differences in history and cultural origins are much too varied for such a narrow application.

During the early to mid 1900s, the concept of family in both the rural south and the major northern cities included any and all people in the community between which there existed a biological or emotional bond. This also included people who simply decided to claim one another as family without the benefit of blood ties. It was in this context of genetic and emotional bonding that the parenting of African American children took place. This community bonding meant that people cared about one another and responded to each individual's needs as if they were blood relatives.

The African American's psychological makeup combined with the social, economic, political, and domestic times fostered this type of family definition and bonding. The uniqueness of the African American experience distinguished its practice of family from the European definition of family. This concept of family in the rural south meant sharing meat from a hog killing or vegetables from the garden with the whole community. In both the north and the south it meant taking care of one another when there was sickness or death. It meant watching out for and even disciplining other's children when necessary. Family meant sharing a set of values and embracing the Christian religion. The idea of seeing a child doing wrong or getting into trouble and not responding to that situation in a corrective manner was unthinkable. The child belonged to the community.

There are those who are advocating a return to this kind of community parenting. While the concept of an inclusive community family is as good today as it was in years past, current conditions preclude its success today. The emotional bonding born out of a need for social, economic, and spiritual survival has been lost. Assimilation or pseudo-assimilation renders it for all purposes extinct.

Recently in Dallas, Texas, a group of Muslims apprehended and whipped two African American teenage boys who were caught burglarizing a local business. The reaction of the African American community to the corporal punishment of these boys was polarized. One segment applauded the action of the Muslims. They said it was a noble thing adhering to the once-held practice of parenting children. This response was consistent with yesteryear when children belonged to the community.

Another segment viewed the boys' action as a criminal offense to be duly treated as such and handled by the proper authorities. Ultimately, the Muslims were not indicted for their actions by the Dallas County District Attorney.

The action of the men was a solid alternative to arrest. The beating may well have saved the boys from a life of crime. The entire episode was perhaps most sobering to those of us who are Christians. We are well aware that many young African Americans lack the skills and ability to live well. Our children tend to aspire to live high without the ability to live skillfully.

PART 1

PARENTING PRINCIPLES FROM THE BOOK OF PROVERBS

Chapter 1

Spiritual Bankruptcy

Proverbs contains a collection of sayings which, using comparison and contrast, set forth spiritual truths. Those specifically germane to parenting are found in chapter four, verses 1-24.

> Hear, O sons, the instruction of a father,
> And give attention that you may gain understanding,
> For I give you sound teaching;
> Do not abandon my instruction.
> When I was a son to my father,
> Tender and the only son in the sight of my mother,
> Then he taught me and said to me,
> "Let your heart hold fast my words;
> Keep my commandments and live;
> Acquire wisdom! Acquire understanding!
> Do not forget, nor turn away from the words of my mouth.
> Do not forsake her, and she will guard you;
> Love her and she will watch over you.
> The beginning of wisdom is: Acquire wisdom;
> And with all your acquiring, get understanding.
> Prize her and she will exalt you;
> She will honor you if you embrace her.
> She will place on your head a garland of grace;
> She will present you with a crown of beauty."
> Proverbs 4:1-9

PARENTING IN THE CONTEXT OF A SPIRITUAL DEFICIT

This section of Proverbs begins by setting forth three basic principles for parenting. First, children who fail at life may be reflecting the spiritual bankruptcy of their forefathers (vv. 1-4). Second, children can only learn the value of a dollar after they understand the value of life (vv. 5-6). Third, children equipped with skills to earn a living, apart from the wisdom to live skillfully, are doomed to fail (vv. 7-9).

PRINCIPLE ONE: CHILDREN WHO FAIL AT LIFE MAY BE REFLECTING THE SPIRITUAL BANKRUPTCY OF THEIR FOREFATHERS (VV. 1-4)

In Proverbs 4, insight is given into the family life of King Solomon. Solomon, the author of this text, invites readers into the home in which he grew up. He was the son of King David, the greatest king the nation of Israel ever had apart from Jesus, their Messiah.

The instructions in this passage about parenting are the instructions of an ethnic father to his ethnic son, growing up in a predominantly pagan religious world. The objective of the lesson is to provide instruction that will enable one to live skillfully and succeed in obtaining and living the good life. Solomon relates what his father told him about how to live skillfully.

David told Solomon that the principles he wished to instill did not originate with him but rather were rooted in the sound and fertile soil of the historical experiences of his father and his father before him (Prov. 4:2). In other words, David said that these principles had been tested in the context of changing times and changing circumstances, in the lives of his predecessors. He admonishes, "Hear, O sons, the instructions of a father, and give attention that you may gain understanding, for I give you sound teaching" (vv. 1-2a).

In using the term "sound teaching" David was emphasizing what he was saying about life and how to live it well was not something that he created himself. They were not instructions of a first generation Christian father trying to do a new thing. Instead these were God-focused ideas and principles; not just notions about God and life that he was making up as he went along. What he was sharing were sound teachings that had stood the test of time and changing circumstances. To put it still another way David was saying that he had lived long enough to see a lot of people, ideas, and principles come and go. But these God-focused principles and ideas about life that he was passing on to him had not only lasted but they had served well those who embraced them.

It is my contention that today's failing children in the African American community are not privy to the sound God-focused teaching that David passed on to Solomon. Thus many of today's children are reflections of the spiritual bankruptcy of their parents. There is a serious deficit of God-focused ideas and principles in the lives of many African American parents.

Various sociological reports and statistics reflect the unprecedented number of African American children who are in trouble all over our country today. We are looking at children who are reflections of a bankrupt spiritual family situation. This bankruptcy is rooted in the loss of a spiritual heritage that used to be passed on from one generation to the next. The sons and daughters of the Civil Rights Movement have grown what may well be called a "cut flower generation." This is a generation of people who do not have their own social stem and root; they can only exist as an extension of their parents. The cut flower generation has no spiritual heritage to embrace.

The spiritual heritage of the African American community was lost in the social, political, and economic transition that resulted from the Civil Rights Movement a few generations ago. It can be argued that the last generation to reflect the rich spiritual heritage of the African American community was the generation born in the 1930s and 1940s, growing up in the 1950s. It was this generation that led the Civil Rights Movement and who today lead in the social, religious, economic, and political arenas. Sadly the average African American youth has little to no awareness of their rich spiritual heritage.

Many of my generation feel an urgency to try to do something to compensate for this deficit. We feel that time is running out for us as a race. When we see the immorality, hear about the violence, and witness the hopelessness we wonder, "Where has our negligence brought us?"

In Deuteronomy 6:20, God said that the time would come when Jewish sons snd daughters would want to know what the testimonies, statutes, and judgments meant that they saw their parents practicing. This would be the opportune time for their parents to teach them about Him and the history of His relationship with them. As a people we have failed to teach our children the God-focused principles inherent in our rich spiritual heritage.

Today, African American children and youth are in many instances quite well off economically. These children are the primary beneficiaries of the upward mobility of their parents. However, many of these same children have serious spiritual deficiencies in their lives. For the most part, if any one of them looked either to the early part of their parents' lives and even to their grandparents' lives they would find little evidence of a genuine spiritual commitment to the living God. There are too few models of what it means to have a relationship with the living God. To live in the context of a spiritual deficit is to live without absolutes or boundaries where everything is relative. Spiritual symbols such as the church may be in place but they lack meaning in the marketplace.

When it came time to exposing our children to good role models, Betty and I had to make some decisions that were not popular with our families. There were family gatherings that we opted not to attend. We didn't want our children to emulate relatives whose spiritual commitment and agendas differed radically from our own. We also did not leave our children in the care of those who were not committed to God-focused spiritual principles.

Bill and Mary were a happy couple, seriously committed to each other and involved in the ministry of the local church. Each summer they sent their two children to the country to spend time with their grandparents. As the children grew older it became evident to Bill and Mary that the influence of their parents and siblings, who were not serious about their relationship with the Lord, was overruling the spiritual principles they were trying to instill in their children. Children are hard-pressed to accept as wrong that which their grandparents embrace as right. The moral attitudes of aunts and uncles may seem acceptable to children even though they differ from what the children are taught at home.

When David told Solomon to pay attention so that he would gain understanding from sound doctrine, he was saying something that few African American parents can say today. Many of us are first-generation believers in the sense that we are serious about living what we believe about our Savior, as opposed to being mere church members. So when we teach our sons and our daughters biblical principles, we find them listening but often with a great deal of suspicion. Many times children hold what their Christian parents say to them about God-focused principles and values in suspect because in reality their parents are the exception to the rule in their extended family.

When a Christian parent talks to his or her child about biblical principles the child listens but often there is little subsequent evidence that they believed what is being said. Children seem to have serious questions as to whether these principles are relevant for today and will produce the same positive results in their lives as in their parents' lives.

Children genuinely think that if they do what their parents say, they will fail. In the experience of the child, their Christian parents' life choices and values were not embraced by their grandparents. Thus as far as today's youth are concerned, the principles being taught are untested, and therefore may not produce the same results in their lives as it did in their parents' lives.

In addition to the struggle of having to parent in a spiritual vacuum as it pertains to one's extended family, oftentimes there are many chaotic situations in the lives of Christian parents that are reflections of their bad choices. These situations echo the absence of wisdom in the lives of the parent. The child begins to wonder, "Are you sure you believe this stuff about God?"

Marriage is a good example of this. We believe that a monogamous relationship is God's choice for parenting and companionship. Yet when our children look back in history, how appealing does our marriage relationship look to them? Suppose your son or daughter is looking at your marriage and family life. Based on what they see in the home, would they recognize God's wisdom? Or would they say that what their parents have is a reflection of a divine wisdom that they are better off without?

Solomon said that in his home he felt like a son to his father (Prov. 4:3). His words were, "When I was a son to my father. . . " King David, although running the whole kingdom of Israel, invested the time and energy to make Solomon feel like his son. David must have made a practice of listening to his son. He treated him with pride and compassion. David esteemed his son highly. There are a lot of children who cannot say that about their fathers. A lot of children cannot say, "My father treats me like a son or a daughter. My father is glad that I am his." This is about nurture which makes a difference in how a child grows up.

Solomon also said that his mother treated him with so much tenderness she made him feel like he was her only son. A lot of children can't say that about their relationship with their mother. From Solomon's perspective, in the heart of his mother he was so precious and tender that he always felt like he was her only son.

There are many homes in which there are deficits. Fathers do not talk to their children; and mothers do not have time for them either. This is a tragic fact. It is possible to have a family that is well-fed, well-housed, well-clothed, and still have a home in which there is a serious spiritual deficit. When children have enough food to eat, clothes to wear, and a house to stay in, that does not mean that they have the spiritual context in which they can be taught wisdom. Solomon said the reason his father could teach him wisdom was because the environment in the home was conducive to it.

Deficits in the home environment and bankruptcy in spiritual heritage are weak fibers that contribute to failure among African American children today.

Wisdom is a virtue that is passed from parent to child and heart to heart, not just head to head. African American Christian parents must be about the business of raising wise children—not simply academically smart, but wise. Parents need to be able to go heart to heart, not just head to head. Parents who talk about teaching their children wisdom need to start with the context in which the child lives. There must be an environment in which hearts are free to operate and positive feelings evident. The child must be able to know and say, "I know you love me. You treat me like I am somebody. I am precious in your sight. I am valuable to you. Your presence makes me feel secure. Your attitude towards me gives me a sense of belonging. I feel your compassion and concern." It is in this environment that it is possible for a parent to teach wisdom to a child.

Betty and I both grew up in an era in the United States in which being black meant being treated as a "nigger" at best. It meant being denied access to life on a level equal with whites. Models of significance portrayed by the media and the entertainment industry were white. Amos and Andy and Steppin Fetchit were intentionally negative models of African American men. Yet we developed into adults who could function in any context socially, economically and educationally. The difference in how Betty and I turned out as adults is the difference parents make when they demonstrate love and affection to their children. In my home I was a son to my father and my mother treated me as if I was her only child. The same was true with Betty and her family.

It was the tender love of Solomon's mother that made him feel like he was her only son. His mother made him feel like the only child, but it was his father who taught him wisdom. His mother set the environment in the home that made the son feel so loved that it was possible for David to teach spiritual convictions. So it must be in every home. The environment must be right in order for the father to teach God-focused principles.

God delegates the teaching and training of a son to the boy's father. This is not to the exclusion of his mother. He does, however, put squarely on the shoulders of the father the responsibility of training his son—to teach him how to live and to give him the proper life values.

The mother has the responsibility of doing the same thing with her daughter (but also not to the exclusion of that girl's father). Titus 2 charges older women to teach younger woman to love their children.

The 1987 issue of "The State of Black America," published annually by the National Urban League in New York, noted that the hope of correcting the crisis of teenage pregnancies can no longer be found in the church. Apparently the author of this article did not believe that the African American church today offers anything relevant to youth. Sadly I am increasingly inclined to agree with this and other similar assessments.

If we evaluate what we are doing in the church and in the home, the evidence suggests that unless we change our attitude and our actions towards that which is spiritual, we will not make a difference in this generation of African American children. Until fathers communicate to their sons that they want to spend quality time with them, there will be no change in the character of the men we raise.

PRINCIPLE TWO: CHILDREN CAN ONLY LEARN THE VALUE OF A DOLLAR AFTER THEY UNDERSTAND THE VALUE OF LIFE (VV. 5-6)

Something strange is happening among today's African American children. I was visiting with a third-grade class at a local elementary school. There were about 30 students in that class and it was my task to explain what I did as a pastor. As I was talking to these students, I asked them what they wanted to be when they grew up. One little boy in particular caught my attention as he aggressively sought to be the first to respond. "I want to be rich," he said. I asked him, "How much money would you like to earn?" He answered, "About three hundred billion dollars." "What would you do with all that money?" I asked. "Buy me a Corvette" he responded. "And what would you do with the rest of your money?" I asked, to which the nine-year old boy had no answer. He never said a word after that, but he knew he wanted a car.

Most children today have learned to consider money as the most important and valuable commodity anyone can possess. If you have money most children think you have all you need. What troubles me is that they believe this even though they may have no idea as to what to do with their money beyond buying cars, recreational gadgets, and clothes.

Most African American parents do not realize that if they gave $30,000 to their children most would find the nearest car dealership and pay the sticker price for a car. If they had money left over, they would have no idea what to do with the rest of it. It would never occur to them that a car might be the least of their needs.

In Proverbs 4:5, David commands his son to acquire wisdom and understanding. Wisdom is the ability to distinguish between that which seems to be important but is not and that which seems not to be important but really is. The command is to acquire wisdom. Wisdom is not something a child is born with. Wisdom and understanding are both acquired. No matter their race or culture, people are not born wise. It is possible to have all kinds of credentials and not be wise. Education, no matter how comprehensive, does not make one wise. Wisdom must be acquired in time and through experience.

There is no question that modern-day parents are telling their children to acquire money and more money, and they will be successful. Money has become a primary focus, even among Christians. What we fail to comprehend as believers is that he who has the skill to acquire money but lacks wisdom is destined to misuse the money because he is ill-equipped to distinguish between that which is important and that which is not. Parents must vocalize often and show by example what is important in life. Most parents simply say, "Get money!"

I often talk about my family because they, along with myself, are subjects by which hypotheses can be tested. One of my theories is that most youngsters do not comprehend the value of a dollar. For example, when accompanied by me, my children will shop at stores with quality merchandise. When shopping on their own, they frequent discount establishments looking for a deal. I contend that "expensive" equals quality—most of the time. But my children only go along with this if they are with me. I do not think that we as parents are successful at teaching our children the value of life. Therefore, they have a less than acceptable comprehension of the value of a dollar.

There are many male African American professional athletes who make large sums of money over a relatively short period of time, and yet few of these men retire with any money at all. Why? I am convinced that the answer lies behind the fact that these men have little to no practical understanding of the value of a dollar. No one has taken the time to teach them what to value in life. By the time they discover what life is about, their money and career are gone. How terribly tragic. Wisdom is the ability to live life skillfully. It is the ability to take hold of life with the skill of an artist or a craftsman and carve out a life that is both fulfilling and satisfying.

The history of African Americans in this country encompasses a legacy of slavery, oppression, and disenfranchisement. There are few African Americans who can say that their success is due to the ideal situations in which they grew up. Every economically successful African American is like all African Americans in this country. Life was dealt to them like a hand of cards. They played it with wisdom as a tool and carved out a successful life. It is interesting to note that most of the national African American leaders of today were born in the 1930s and 40s and grew up in the 50s when everything was stacked against them.

Wisdom is the ability to make wise choices and wise choices are made by understanding issues and the values that are involved. Understanding the value of life means being clear who God is. Wisdom allows a person to distinguish between good and evil. A wise person looks at a situation and can readily recognize either good or evil. Wisdom promises to guard, protect, and watch over those who are devoted and loyal to it. That is exactly what many parents are telling children that money will do for them. Wisdom says, "I will guard you. If you don't forsake me, I will guard you. If you love me, I will watch over you." Parents communicate to their children that money provides nourishment, clothing, shelter, love, protection—total security.

How does wisdom guard and watch over those who love it? Wisdom does this by dictating the life values and choices of individuals. Wisdom equips and directs a person in choosing and establishing a sound and wholesome value system and lifestyle. In the area of life choices wisdom directs. It enables one to discern between choices that provide immediate gratification and those that have a more lasting result.

A student with wisdom will say of school, "Yes, I could skip class and sleep in, but that would not be wise for me." Wisdom will tell him to make preparations (lessons, clothing, alarm clock) the night before in order to be ready for the next day. A wise person can see more then what is readily evident, more than what is sitting on the table, more than what meets the eye.

I have said that to appreciate the value of a dollar a child must learn the value of life. The prodigal son in Luke 15 is an example of what I mean. In that parable we have the story of a young man who did not understand the value of a dollar because he did not understand the value of life.

SPIRITUAL BANKRUPTCY

The prodigal son evidenced no knowledge of who God is or why he was created, thus he acted accordingly. He told his father that he didn't have time to wait until he died. As one of two sons who would inherit an equal share of the estate, he wanted his portion now. The father complied.

The young man took all that his father gave him, and made every effort to remove himself from his father's seemingly restrictive authority. To this end he not only left home but he left the country, and with gusto he proceeded to spend everything he had. When his money ran out his lifestyle sank to the level of swine in a pigpen. Without food and a place to stay, hunger drove him to a pig farm where his menu consisted of hog slop. It was at this degrading level of subsistence that he experienced a radical change in his attitude about the nature of life. As he began to grasp the meaning of life, the authority of his father did not seem quite so restrictive.

The difference between a prodigal son and one who is no longer a prodigal is one of perception and perspective—one has insight and the other lacks discernment. One views things in their right relations; the other has tunnel vision. One son is a spendthrift, while the other manages finances well. The prodigal has no sense of the meaning of life and thus has an unhealthy view of money. The son who is no longer a prodigal has learned the value of life and recast his priorities so that his highest value is on wisdom not money.

There are too many fathers who are willing to let their sons "find themselves' in life's pigpens. All children do not come back from dining at pig troughs. They instead develop a taste for pigsties. These rebellious children will forever be among swine, eating like them, smelling like them, living like them, and acting like them.

An example of a wise young man was Solomon. God answered Solomon's prayer to grant him wisdom rather than riches. He said, "Because you have asked this thing and have not asked for yourself long life, nor have asked riches for yourself, nor have you asked for the life of your enemies, but have asked for yourself discernment to understand justice, behold, I have done according to your words. Behold, I have given you a wise and discerning heart, so that there has been no one like you before you, nor shall one like you arise after you" (1 Kings 3:11-12).

The greatest thing a child can acquire is not money but wisdom. Evidence attests to the fact that it is not the lack of money that is causing our children to fail. Many children who are prone to violence are the sons and daughters of middle class African Americans. The primary contributing factor to the trouble our children are in today is the absence of wisdom.

Principle Three: Children Equipped with the Skills to Make Money but without Wisdom Quickly Fail (vv. 7-49)

From the window of my office at the Institute for Black Family Renewal in Dallas, Texas, I often see teenaged men and women making money by buying and selling crack cocaine and other illegal drugs to people of all races and social classes. These young people work shifts twenty-four hours a day. They even have curbside service for those who are passing through in a hurry on their way to work.

It is obvious that these young men and women are equipped with the skill to make money but the nature of their work suggests that they lack the wisdom to live skillfully. The evidence of this absence of wisdom can be seen in the fragmented lives that characterize every area of their lives.

As mentioned earlier, Solomon is an example of a young man well equipped to make money but who lacked the wisdom to reign successfully as king of Israel. In humble recognition of his lack of wisdom, Solomon asked God for that very thing so that he would be able to reign wisely.

Jacob is another example of a man who had the skill to make money but also was not equipped to live skillfully. In searching for ways to make money, Jacob turned to his mother who taught him how to prioritize his own self-interests, even at the expense of other people. Throughout most of his life, Jacob evidenced the kind of character that repeatedly saw him getting what he wanted from others, at the sad expense of developing the skills that would enable him to live wisely and well. He turned every relationship into one of conflict and hostility. In him we see one of the primary negative virtues inherent in the skill to make money apart from the skill to live wisely. That is the ability to practice deception in order to manipulate a person or situation to get what he wanted.

Thus when Jacob wanted his brother's birthright, he used his ability to be deceptive to cheat his brother out of it. And if that wasn't enough, he deceived his aged father and stole his brother's blessing. Later, he cheated his father-in-law to get rich.

Jacob's lack of wisdom not only caused him to have trouble at home, but it also seemed to cause trouble wherever he went, causing him considerable unhappiness. He had to flee from his home to save his life and his deceptive ways also interfered with his romance with Rachel.

In parenting, the priority must consistently be placed on living skillfully rather than on simply making money. Children who arrive at adulthood without the skills to live wisely are destined to fail in their attempts to live life well. In Genesis 47:9, Jacob describes his life as having been a failure. This failure was not evidenced in his lack of material gain for when he died he owned much. Rather, his failure was in his inability to develop and maintain positive relationships with others.

As was the case with Jacob, today's children who learn how to get what they want at the expense of others have learned how to make money but they have not learned how to live skillfully. And like Jacob, these children are unhappy and unfulfilled in their lives, quite often lacking any positive relationships, even in their own home. A child equipped with the ability to make money but not to live wisely is equipped to fail.

Chapter 2

THE PRIORITY: SPIRITUALITY

Parents are charged with the responsibility of providing for the needs of their progeny. It could be argued that African American parents go the extra mile to meet their children's social, physical, educational, emotional, and psychological needs. Social clubs, sororities, fraternities, and other organizations abound. The most nutritious food, regular checkups, and sports activities are a given. Competition for the best grades, academic recognition and acceptance at the most prestigious university begins early. Anything that may raise or maintain the child's self-esteem and contribute to his or her emotional and psychological stability is done, including pageants, praise, toys, cars, electronic gadgets, designer clothes, and then more toys. Placed in the proper perspective, none of these things are wrong. My contention, however, is that the priority in parenting should be on spiritual development.

In Proverbs 1:7, David told Solomon that the beginning of knowledge is the acquisition of wisdom. No one is born wise. It does not come with years of education or the earning of degrees. Parents cannot wish it on their children. They can, however, pray that God will give their children a taste for wisdom. To this end God will grant parents the ability to create that taste. Wisdom is the ability to make wise choices. It makes one cognizant of the fact that actions taken today will have to be lived with

THE PRIORITY: SPIRITUALITY

tomorrow. The individual must personally desire wisdom and be willing to strive to obtain it.

Proverbs 1:7 also tells us, "The fear of the Lord is the beginning of knowledge; fools despise wisdom and instruction." This fear of God is an attitude of reverence for and awe toward God. This reverence and awe compels one to strive to obey God.

Creating a taste for wisdom begins early in the believer's life. The parents are the primary teachers, but instruction may come from other sources. Sunday school teachers make Bible characters come to life using age-appropriate materials. VBS, youth camps, clubs, choirs, and other programs can help to create a thirst for knowledge. I have observed the eagerness with which children embrace things that are spiritual only to lose interest over time. In my experience as a pastor, it appears that the older children get, the less inclined they are toward spiritual things. Some become cynical, refusing to listen to God's word. Other listen half-heartedly, preferring to be elsewhere. A precious few continue to demonstrate a desire for wisdom. Since this is true in the vast majority of cases I have encountered, I conclude that to the extent that our children abandon their faith in the living God, to that extent they show themselves to be lacking in wisdom. To that extent they are also headed toward lives that are failures.

There is a direct relationship between a young person's walk with God and his or her corresponding performance in areas of accountability at home, in school, or in the place of employment. One can be counted on to complete household chores without complaining; the other doesn't see why he should be given any chores at all. After all, it isn't his house. One child studies hard and exceeds his potential; the other, although gifted, doesn't take studies seriously and fails. At the work place, one youth does everything as unto the Lord; the other falls short and compensates by "brown-nosing."

Many parents have brought their younger children to me for counseling. They were failing in school and the parents said that they didn't know why. It is my contention that they *did* know. They knew their child did not love Jesus. They knew that child hated church and detested that which was spiritual. They knew that child never prayed and resented having to study the Bible. Why were the parents surprised? They should not have been. They should have been astonished if he had passed.

A former football player recently told me that a growing number of football players are getting saved. He said that they are discovering that money and fame do not give them a satisfying identity nor fill the emptiness in their soul. Many people, regardless of their age, have a desire to be recognized as being somebody significant in life. Most people want to be honored by someone. The question is, how do we achieve such accolades? Is it by being smarter than other people? Is that how we are exalted? Is it a matter of being more daring than others? Is that how we get honored? Do honor and prestige come to those who have the most money and credentials? The answer is no.

To be exalted according to Proverbs 4:8-9 a person must be willing to pay any price for wisdom. David said to Solomon, "Prize her, and she will exalt you; she will honor you if you embrace her" (Prov. 4:8). Have you talked with your children and said to them, "I want you to be wise. I want you to have the skill to live. If you grab hold of wisdom and hug her and embrace her, she will place a garden of grace on your head and a wreath around your head. Wisdom will present you with a crown of beauty."

What is this wisdom? It is knowing God through Jesus Christ. It is the willingness to live each day in obedience to the Word and will of God. That is wisdom. Wisdom begins with knowing God through Jesus Christ. It is the willingness to say, "God, I know what You have said and I am going to do it." Wisdom is having the sense to turn to the Bible and look to God for the answers.

The Rewards: Longevity, Character, Success

Hear, my son, and accept my sayings,
And the years of your life will be many.
I have directed you in the way of wisdom;
I have led you in upright paths.
When you walk, your steps will not be impeded;
And if you run, you will not stumble.
Take hold of instruction; do not let go.
Guard her, for she is your life.
Do not enter the path of the wicked,
And do not proceed in the way of evil men.

THE PRIORITY: SPIRITUALITY

Avoid it, do not pass by it;
Turn away from it and pass on.
For they cannot sleep unless they do evil;
And they are robbed of sleep unless they make some one stumble.
For they eat the bread of wickedness,
And drink the wine of violence.
But the path of the righteous is like the light of dawn,
That shines brighter and brighter until the full day.
The way of the wicked is like darkness;
They do not know over what they stumble.
Proverbs 4:10-19

Parents have the task of creating in their children (individuals 20 years of age and under) a taste for wisdom. If the instructions learned are followed, good decisions are made and they impact life for the better. In Proverbs 4:10-19 the rewards of acquiring wisdom are explored.

First, wisdom promises long life to those who love her. Second, the product of wisdom is character built on integrity. Third, the fruit of wisdom is success.

One day in September a little girl was browsing though a Christmas catalog with her older sister. Her sister pointed out what she wanted Santa to bring her and said that she would be glad when Christmas came. The younger sibling eagerly inquired, "When is Christmas coming?" The older girl replied, "Oh, in about three months." To which the younger remarked, "Oh, goody!" Predictably, every day in the following weeks was met with the inquiry, "Is Christmas here yet?" It would be unusual to find a preschooler who has an accurate perception of time.

I am not an avid fan of of talk shows. The guest, however, can provide some startling insights into the thoughts that young black Americans have. The following examples are excerpts relating to life and time:

"I'm going to get me mine now."
"I'm too young to wait."
"Tomorrow ain't promised . . . "
"College takes too long."
"I don't think about next year."

Many older children, like the preschooler, have a skewed perception of time. The idea of living a long life is neither relevant nor appealing. With no vision for tomor-

Parenting In The Context Of A Spiritual Deficit

row they can only see logic in simply being consumers. Why plan for a career now that will ensure a good retirement? These youths can't see 10, 15 or 20 years into the future. Don't even mention 50 years! I often tell couples who come to me for counseling that he or she wouldn't treat the other so carelessly if they realized they could be living with this person another fifty years.

One of the rewards of wisdom is longevity. These young people no doubt can see value in delaying immediate gratification and deferring to plans for the long haul. If we are to believe what we hear and view via the airwaves or read in print, we can conclude that possessions, not character, determine a person's worth. Some of the people held in the highest esteem are entertainers, actors, athletes, drug dealers, and pimps who are known for making lots of money and are notorious for living shabby lives. These are the role models of our impressionable youths.

Young people who have wisdom have direction. They know that character built on integrity will stand them in good stead at home, school, and in the work place. The child who is wise will experience success. He has made good choices and will reap the reward of skillful living. The child who detests instruction has the desire to live high, but can't apart from parental support. He is like a flower that only blooms when connected to the root of the plant. Once the flower is cut, it withers. So it is with many of today's youth. They are members of the "cut flower" generation that lacks roots to support themselves.

As children begin to enter into adulthood they begin to develop a sense of tomorrow. We must teach our children that what they are characterwise is much more important than what they own. Our children must come to understand that for those who have wisdom to live skillfully, there is for them the promise of a good, long life.

Choosing The Right Path: The Choice Of Champions

With the use of the imagery of thoroughfares, Proverbs 4:14-19 describes life in terms of values, goals, and destiny. The wicked who thrive on evil deeds are fated to have short lives. The better path promises long life in God's favor. It is important to convey to every child the idea that they are always headed somewhere in life. Wisdom will

THE PRIORITY: SPIRITUALITY

teach children how to choose good and how to get there.

With wisdom one can see the differences between the various alternatives. To entice the traveler to choose a path of wisdom, wisdom offers the traveler the promise of a long life. It is my contention that the desire to live a long life is the primary source of motivation for a child to want to choose the path of right and righteousness. The person who has no hope of a tomorrow has nothing on the inside of their heart and mind to which the parents can appeal for motivation to delay immediate self- gratification.

As long as a young person has no hope of a tomorrow he or she will have no reason to plan for it today. The absence of hope is a primary reason why many young people put everything on the line for what they feel at the moment. It is the responsibility of parents to teach them differently. It is the promise of tomorrow that wisdom uses to entice the young traveler to choose the path of wisdom.

Today there is an increasing number of young grandmothers. One reason is that many mothers have stopped helping their daughters make good life decisions. Today youth have no reason to do or not to do something because life is all a matter of relative choices based on what they feel at the moment. This is a dangerous way to live. Wisdom say to the youth, if you choose me I promise to equip you with the tools to live a long quality life.

A long life is a life lived on the path of righteousness in which there is freedom to move. When I talk about the path of righteousness I am talking about character—the kind of Christian a person is. A person of character is one who knows the difference between being and owning. This is the kind of person for whom doing right has strong appeal. The Bible says seek first the kingdom of heaven and God's righteousness and He will add everything else. If you were to paraphrase that you could say if you choose to have Jesus Christ in you heart when you are young you will not grow up with skeletons in your closet. You will not make decisions today that you will regret tomorrow.

PAYDAY SOMEDAY: THE POWER OF WINNERS

Wisdom also builds character. According to the Bible the normal life span of a person is between seventy and eighty years (Ps. 90). If you take those years and divide them into four sections of twenty each, one could make the argument that an increasing number of our young people have wasted their lives before they have even finished one-fourth of their normal life span. This means that many of those young people who have not been killed before they turn twenty-five will live some sixty or more years of their lives in a state of total failure. A young person who has failed at life as a teen has little reason to value living.

In Psalm 90:12, in view of the lifespan a person will normally live the psalmist pleads, "Lord, teach me to number my days that I may present to Thee a heart of wisdom." In other words, let every day count. In Psalm 39:4 in view of the temporal nature of life the plea is, "Lord, make me know my end and the extent of my days." The psalmist says, I am going to be around awhile. I want to make it count. And he says, I know I won't stay here forever so I want to make it count. These passages should dictate the kind of character we must have in order to choose for ourselves the path of life that leads to success.

A primary responsibility of all parents is to share with their children that life has a payday. Everybody will receive the fruit of their life choices when payday arrives. There is no escape.

What becomes of old prostitutes? Where do they spend their senior years? They chose a path that caused them to put all that they had on the sex market. What becomes of old pimps? What does he do when he cannot make it on the streets any longer? I watched a pimp grow old. It was a sad sight. I watched a man grow old who had never worked a day in his life and he told me "I want you to know that every girl I ever put on the street, I got her out of the church. They were the best kind." I watched him die as a man of bad choices. He never accepted Christ as his Savior.

What happens to those who cannot read and write? Is there a place for the broken and battered people who only know how to hurt others? What do you do if you have ruled your world by your fists and you can no longer see?

Jim was a man who ruled his family with his fist. He beat his children and his wife at will. Fear was evident in the lives of Jim's children. I watched Jim grow old and as he aged his ability to rule with his fist slowly diminished. In time Jim could no longer move fast enough to dominate his family with his fist, so he would strike at them with his walking cane. Jim evidently concluded that he would always be the strong black giant of a man that he was in his youth. Jim was wrong in this. Time stole his youth and his strength abandoned him to the fruit of his life choices. Jim's payday came and it was sad.

This world does not emphasize aging and the fruit of bad choices. Young people need to see how those are living with the fruit of their lives, whether good or bad. Without wisdom there is no room for integrity. The product of wisdom is character built on integrity. It is not possible to collect a good payday from a bad investment.

LEARNING FROM THE HOOD: DANCING WITH DANGER

Paul wrote to the Corinthians, "bad company corrupts good morals" (1 Cor. 15:33). This passage makes the point that when a person chooses to associate with people who do evil, in time the fruit of evil will become appealing. That makes doing evil more exciting, satisfying, fulfilling, and beneficial than doing what is right.

Many youth in the church have been seduced by the fruits of evil. They think that the righteous behavior of their parents is due to their age, not commitment to Christ. There is to them a more exciting way to live. It is called evil but they call it fun. The question is what's wrong with the way they live? Proverbs 4:15. Avoid the appeal that evil has to your old nature. Don't go near it.

Wisdom also says recognize that there are people who are wicked and evil and such people have a strong propensity towards doing what is evil. They not only do evil but they live to do evil. They eat the bread of wickedness and drink the wine of violence. In other words, they get high off of doing wrong. And they will entice your sons and your daughters to do the same. To company with such people is to dance with danger in the hood.

Many children have a serious deficit in their character because they tend to hang out with the worst of people in the hood. Survey your children's friends. Ask what might cause them to associate with the wrong people. We have this idea that if our children get into trouble it was someone else's fault. But the truth is the child chose to hang out with the wrong crowd because they wanted to.

Parents need to be asking the hard questions of their

children: Why do the worst of people appeal to you? Why are you spending time with kids who are on drugs? Why are all your friends flunking in school? What's wrong with them? These choices reflect a deficit in character.

It bothers me that often the worse people of the community are more attractive to our youth than are the best people. I said to my daughter, "Your mother is the best woman God made. Why would you choose somebody else to imitate who does not even go to church?" It may surprise you to find out that you are not your son's hero. Could it be that our young people like what we have but are unimpressed with what we are? I am convinced that most of our children do not view us as having succeeded in life. I am talking about us as parents. Our children are looking around for someone who in their eyes has succeeded. Our own children are often unimpressed with what we are.

At the welfare office there are many young women with two or more babies. Many of them are not even twenty years old yet. A girl who had a child at thirteen will most likely have one or two more before she is twenty, many times with a different father for each one. So she sits at the welfare office looking for some help. Realize that for the next forty years she will be doing that. By the time those children are near grown, she will most likely have their children to raise.

In the local jails there are too many young men bargaining away their future. When a person is arrested in any large city, justice does not take place in the courthouse. A lawyer will talk to the district attorney's office who sets in motion a plea bargain.

In the communities on the corner, there are too many idle men who do nothing but hang around. They did not work last year, this year, and will not be working next year. That is largely because many of these men never learned to read and write. That corner they hang around on is going to get very stale over the next forty years.

These are young people who are just stumbling around in the dark, groping for life. They have yet to discover as Proverbs 4:18 states that the path of the righteous is described as a breaking of dawn and the light just gets brighter. The path of the righteous is like the light of dawn that shines brighter and brighter until the full day.

There are some things that are essential for any per-

THE PRIORITY: SPIRITUALITY

son who wants to succeed. One such thing is a taste for righteousness. A desire to hang out with the right folks and do the right thing. Parent, you cannot choose the company your son or your daughter keeps. Righteousness is spurned in our day and as a result of that many children are stumbling around in the dark. The difference that righteousness makes in a person's life is the difference between stumbling in the dark and walking in the light.

When I was in seminary, I watched men who were intent on studying the original languages, which were difficult for me. I just started praying, Lord, give me the ability to learn Greek and please, Lord, give me the ability to learn Hebrew. And God did that for me.

Several things about the prodigal son in Luke 15 bear considering. First, this young man had the character of a possessor. He said to his father, give me what is mine. I want it now. It never occurred to him that though he was bold and tough enough to demand what was his, he lacked the wisdom to manage either himself or his share of the estate. He did not have that character. In a very short time this young man went from a palace, to the streets, and finally to a pigpen. He went from having everything to having nothing. He lacked wisdom. The Bible says this young man squandered his estate with loose living. He was the kind of young man to whom life in the fast lane was appealing. He had money to spend and did not have the good sense to spend it well. He had no vision of tomorrow so he spent and spent until he had nothing left to spend. Then all of his friends left him. And just to survive he went to care for pigs to live, and he ate what the pigs were eating. The Bible says in the pigpen he came to his senses. He realized he had a rich father and he was eating with the pigs.

It is good to be able to know the difference between life in a pigpen and life in a palace. That is a good distinction to be able to make but too many young people today, are heading to the pigpen.

People who cannot read and write have made a choice already. The good news is this: If you are tired of what you are doing with your life, if today you are living in the pigpen of failure, there is an alternative to that. And that alternative is Jesus Christ and His righteousness. I would submit to you today that it is a good thing to know when to start over. Today would be the best day to do that.

Chapter 3

The Key: Skillful Living

The principle in this section, living skillfully, is the key to physical, emotional, and spiritual wholeness. By wholeness I have in mind a person who develops into adulthood with their spirit, mind, and muscles all in sync with each other. There are three points in this section that I will underscore. First, teach children how to live skillfully and they will know the secret of good health. Second, teach children how to protect their hearts from deception and they will not be fragmented emotionally. Third, teach a child how to avoid goal-altering distractions and they will learn how to accomplish their life goals.

> My son, give attention to my words;
> Incline your ear to my sayings.
> Do not let them depart from your sight;
> Keep them in the midst of your heart.
> For they are life to those who find them,
> And health to all their whole body.
> Watch over your heart with all diligence,
> For from it flow the springs of life.
> Put away from you a deceitful mouth,
> And put devious lips far from you.
> Let your eyes look directly ahead,
> And let your gaze be fixed straight in front of you.
> Watch the path of your feet,

THE KEY: SKILLFUL LIVING

And all your ways will be established.
Do not turn to the right nor to the left;
Turn your foot from evil (Prov. 4:20-27).

One would think that in the context of a society such as ours in which physical fitness is the watchword on the lips of the old and young alike, that it would be totally unnecessary to talk about spiritual, physical, and emotional wholeness. However, the high level of drug and alcohol abuse among young people, the fast food diets that make up the nutrition of young children, combined with a high number of children who are in therapy today, all suggest that such an emphasis is more than necessary.

The point I am focusing on is that physical and emotional health is inherent to one who has wisdom. Thus the focus here is not on acquired street smarts or basic survival skills, but on the importance of emphasizing good health as an essential element in skillful living.

In speaking to the issue of living skillfully in terms of learning the secret of good health, let me define wisdom as the ability to carve out for oneself a life that is based on righteousness in attitude, habits and in general lifestyle. Such a life lends itself to the pursuit and acquisition of success. The Bible says, "Seek first the kingdom of God and His righteousness, and all else will be added" (my paraphrase).

A wise young person is one who under the teaching of their parents has acquired a taste for a quality life and in the process of growing up in a positive home environment has developed a sense as to where to find that which is classified as the good life. A child who has a genuine taste for a positive, quality life in both their present and their future has a sense of how to attain that quality life that they hunger for.

To say that skillful living is the key to physical and emotional wholeness is to suggest a second principle. Teach your children how to protect their hearts from deception and they will not be fragmented emotionally. It has long been my observation that parents tend to give too little attention to the emotional development of their children. Thus many children reach adulthood who are seriously handicapped emotionally.

To understand this point, it is necessary to establish a

PARENTING IN THE CONTEXT OF A SPIRITUAL DEFICIT

profile of a child who is alive in his or her spirit, healthy in mind, and whole in body. Such a young person has the ability to enjoy the freedom and pleasures of youth with a firm heart commitment to Jesus Christ. This heart commitment is most evident in the child's attitude toward the child's parents.

A child whose heart is being protected by his or her parents is one who enjoys the freedom of their childhood and their youth. This means growing up in an environment in which there is the option to act the part of a child and enjoy the pleasure of being a teenager.

In summary, a child whose heart is properly protected by the parents is one who develops and maintains a high value on the relationship with God. In addition this young person places a high value on the relationship with their parents.

The young person for whom skillful living is the key is one whose parents apply a third principle. Teach a child how to avoid goal-altering distractions and they will learn how to accomplish their life goals. In my observations of young people over the years, including my own children, it is clear to me that there is a major difference between what distracts boys and what distracts girls.

This difference between male and female distractions is most evident on the college campus among freshmen. The young women arrive on campus with the same cravings that they evidenced in high school, namely, an unquenchable desire for someone to love them and make them feel significant and secure. This craving is epitomized in her vulnerability to sexual exploitation that fragments her emotionally and distracts her from her life goals. The young man on the other hand, longs for something that makes him feel good and significant. This craving for material possessions is most evident in his pursuit of things like cars, parties and sex.

When Billy Jean arrived at the university, she had all of the financial aid she needed to complete her education. The dollar amount of her tuition scholarship bore witness to the fact that Billy was more than a little bit brilliant in terms of her intellect. In addition to being smart, she was also a very beautiful young woman.

The unfortunate reality was that Billy Jean had grown up in a home environment in which her heart had been left exposed to the enticing seductive prowling of the university "lobby lizards." In short, she fell prey to sexual temptations and was subsequently distracted from her goals. She thought she was in love but the young man who had fixed his attentions on her did not feel the same way.

In Proverbs 4:20-27, Solomon sets forth the idea that wisdom says that those who choose her will experience long life with good health. Wisdom promises to teach the young person how to protect the heart from empty affections and life-altering distractions.

Please note that the source from which the child is to obtain the skill in living is their own parents. It says, "My son . . ." (this is father talking to son), "Son, listen to what I'm telling you." I understand the text to be saying that the source, the storehouse that the son shows up and reaches in to get the wisdom to live wisely comes out of the parents' storehouse. It does not come from the school; it does not come from the streets. It does not even come from the church. You cannot teach a kid at church what the parents do not embrace at home. This text is saying that as a parent if I want my child or my children to be together in their head, in their heart, in their life, then I have to raise them like that. And you have to raise yours like that. I want to establish the fact in our minds that it does not happen automatically. You have got to produce such a kid.

It is not unusual to hear parents whose children have gone or are going bad say of that child, I do not know what's wrong with that boy or that girl, they just will not listen to me.

CHAPTER 4

TRAIN UP A CHILD: PREACHING TO THE WIND

The point I have sought to make in part one is that life is filled with choices to be made on a daily basis. Among the many choices that a child must make is which path in life they are going to choose. The role of wisdom in this decision-making process is to entice children to choose it as the road they will travel in route to eternity.

The effectiveness of the appeal of wisdom to the child is dictated by the ability of wisdom to entice the child to choose it. To this end wisdom must find something inside the child to which to appeal. That to which wisdom makes its appeal inside the child is the promise of long life. Thus to the extent a child is persuaded that they have a tomorrow in which they will live, to that extent wisdom will be effective in its appeal to the child to choose it.

Bob's young son made it to his senior year in high school when he lost hope of finishing. The fact was that Bob Jr. had simply quit trying, choosing instead to spend his time sleeping, talking on the phone, and playing video games. To say the least, his parents were frustrated.

It happened that Bob Jr.'s father remembered that his son desperately wanted a new car. He had spoken frequently of his desire for one for several years. The older he got, the more he talked about having his own car. Armed with this desire for a car, Bob's father decided to offer his son a car in exchange for his going to summer school, taking a college course, and working a full-time job, all in that summer. His son responded to his offer with enthusiasm and at summer's end he had succeeded in fulfilling all of his father's expectations. When he returned to high school for his final year, he was driving a new car.

Bob's father simply found a way to create in his son the kind of motivation that could function each day in view of tomorrow's positive goals. For Bob Jr. the prospect of owning his own new car provided such a motivation.

Parents who want their children to choose the path of wisdom must so model wisdom in their own life choices that their children are enticed to choose the same path as their parents did. Simply stated, parents who evidence fragmented lives that have resulted from fragmented life choices are hard-pressed to persuade their children to choose the path of wisdom.

A frequently aired anti-drug television commercial makes my point most clearly. In this commercial, the father discovers his son's drug paraphernalia in his room and he is so angry that he aggressively confronts his son about his drug use. The father demanded to know who taught him how to use drugs. The son then shouts back at his father, "You did!" The response silences the father.

Parents whose life choices do not reflect the grace and beauty of wisdom will find it difficult to entice their children to choose the path of wisdom. In most instances the child will emulate the choices of the parents.

There is an old Hebrew proverb that says that when it happened that a Hebrew woman gave birth to a child that was reluctant to nurse from it's mother, the mother would then crush dates and spread the sweet syrup on her breast. The mother would again try to get the baby to nurse. When the baby tasted the sweet syrup, it would begin to nurse.

So it is with parents who entice their children to choose the path of wisdom. They must model wisdom so that their children can taste the sweetness that results from their lives. It is the sweet taste of wise choices that creates in children a desire to choose the right path.

YOUR FAITH, THEIR FAITH: IS THERE A DIFFERENCE?

I asked a father not long ago in a counseling session, "How long has it been since you noticed that your daughter will not listen to you? How long, sir, has that been?" He said just a few months ago he noticed that she would not pay any attention. It did not matter what he said. I said, "You mean that your daughter just stopped listening to you a few months ago? Is that what you are saying? Am I understanding you correctly? Or do you mean that you just noticed that she was no longer listening to you a few months ago? There is a big difference between the answers to the two questions. Do you mean you just noticed it a few months ago and was it not a few months ago that you noticed that she was in trouble?" And I said, "Let me remind you I know these are hard questions."

Is that how it is with you and your kids? Is it true that you really know what it is that your child believe about right and wrong? Is that how it is? You need to answer that for yourself. Will you only discover how much your child disagrees with your conviction when they get into trouble?

Many of us have no idea how much of what we believe about God and His righteousness that our children also believe. I am afraid that for all too many of us our concept of what's right and wrong is not shared by our children. Parents must be careful not to discover the difference between their convictions and their children's conviction only when their child gets in trouble.

When was the last time you asked the child, "Tell me the truth now, do you really agree with my God-focused convictions?" You see, these are from my storehouse of wisdom, no matter how much or how little wisdom I have in my storehouse. From that storehouse my children must gather sufficient wisdom to carve out for themselves a whole and well-balanced life. They have to get it from my wife and I. They do not have any other place to go but the streets. If there is nothing stored in your house of wisdom then your kids are already in trouble.

It is frightening that mothers know what their children like to eat but they don't know what they think. Teach your children how to live skillfully and they'll know the secret of being a whole and healthy person.

Facing the Facts: What Are We Doing?

How are we doing as parents of African American children? How do we know whether or not our children are getting what they must have to live skillfully from us? If you simply look at the externals, it can look like we are succeeding, but there is another story that must be told.

African American youths have a fifty percent higher probability of dying before age twenty than do white children. The greatest cause of death among white youths are accidents and heart disease. Among black youths the most frequent cause of death is homicide, drug abuse, suicide, and accidents. How are we doing? We are talking about a conspiracy to destroy black kids and who are the conspirators? It may well be that it is us, their parents.

Thirty percent of all black youth in America drop out of school before the ninth grade. Most of these dropouts are boys. Black men live five to ten years less than white men. Women will outlive their husbands by at least five or ten years. Forty-two percent of all the homicide victims in America are African American. Forty-two percent of all the people that are murdered in America are African American. Now blacks comprise just eleven percent of the population. The primary killers of black people are young black people who are twenty-four years of age and younger. How are we doing? There are more African Americans being killed by black people today than the KKK killed in their most influential time period.

How are we doing as parents? The facts say we are not doing well at teaching our children skillful living, how to carve out for themselves a life that is satisfying, whole, and fulfilling. Look around the community and ask the question, who is killing who?

Consider the fact that more African American men are dying of cancer today than ever before. What kind of cancer? Lung cancer due to cigarettes. The easiest cancer to prevent is lung cancer. The highest volume of cigarette advertising is done in black America. Any time you are in a black community look at the signs advertising cigarettes. Do you know who gives more money to the United Negro College Fund than anybody else in America? The tobacco industry. That is why many magazines geared toward the African American market seldom publish articles against tobacco. That is also why the United Negro College Fund, as well as many black college presidents, seldom speak out against cigarette smoking. So we educate a man only to watch him kill himself with cigarettes.

Parenting In The Context Of A Spiritual Deficit

Do you know that the only people in our community who have the independence to speak against this murderous industry is the church? But we cannot do that because our officers smoke. Do you? What are your children learning about good health if you are blowing smoke all over them? Skillful, wise living? No. Unfortunately, the kids are just doing what we do.

Look At The Models: How Are We Doing?

More African American men today are alcoholics than ever before. There are many reasons why they are not being helped but one of the reasons is they refuse help when it is offered. African American men feel like they do not need help. In addition to all of this, African Americans are killing themselves in record numbers. The suicide rate is growing among young black men and women today. The age group that is killing themselves the most is twenty to thirty-four. Now if the key to good health is wisdom, then we are not doing well. Are you the kind of parent that is so exhausted from just trying to get some happiness for yourself that you've got nothing left for your children?

An Endangered Species: Are We Victims Or Villains?

I read an article entitled "Black Men, An Endangered Species: Who's Really Pulling the Trigger?"[1] The authors of that particular article make several recommendations as to how to deal with the problem of failing black men. Of the list of recommendations for solutions listed I was particularly interested in this recommendation: "Black parents should spend more time raising their male children." (Interesting, male children.) "In many families sons do not receive the nurturing their daughters receive. They are allowed too much freedom to decide their lifestyles, educational goals, and careers. As a consequence, many black men never reach their full potential. Black parents, especially fathers, must invest more quality time and energy in raising sons."

---

[1] Thomas Parham and Roderick J. McDavis, "Black Men, An Endangered Species: Who's Really Pulling the Trigger?" *Journal of Counseling and Development* 66 (September 1987), 24-27.

The truth is that often we are doing a good job in raising our daughters, but we are not doing as well in parenting our sons. We force our sons to often grow up before they reach their teens. Poor little fellow is nothing more than a child and yet when he hurts we tell him, "Boy, be tough, don't cry." Somebody hits him on the head with a bat and we say, "Kick them in the chin, but don't cry." I know that feeling because I saw somebody hit my child the other day and I sure wanted to say to my son, "Listen, you're the biggest. Hit them back." I want to tell you my friend, teaching a kid to fight is dangerous today because kids kill kids these days.

CUSTODIAN OF THE HEART: WHO IS GUARDING THE FOUNTAIN OF LIFE?

The father said to his son, "Let your heart hold fast my words." Here again in Proverbs 4:4 we have the same thing. We must understand as parents that wisdom is a skill that is passed from father to son, from heart to heart, not head to head. It is a good thing for a son to know his father loves him. A son needs to hear from his father, "Son, I love you and you mean everything to me. When I am gone I want you to carry on the family spiritual legacy. I want you to reflect my value and the character I built in you."

The fondest memory I have as a fifty-seven-year-old man, married thirty five years, is as a boy sitting in the woodpile with my daddy who could not read and could only write his name as his children taught him to do. That man who was illiterate taught me how to understand people. He had wisdom and he wanted to pass it on to me. My father loved me and he made sure that I knew it. He showed me in every way he could that he loved me. It made a big difference in how I grew up.

Bob and his wife came to me for counseling. I said to Bob, "You know, I suspect you know nothing about how to love your wife because I don't think you know anything about what it means to love." And then I said, "I think you are just like your daddy. Your problem is that your wife is not like your mama." He started crying. He just broke down. What I said to Bob was too close to the truth.

The truth was Bob had never seen love in his home. He never saw his parents hug each other, never heard them

Parenting In The Context Of A Spiritual Deficit

exchange words of love and compassion. And yet his wife expected it of him, but he could not do it. That is true in many of our homes. Our children think we are supposed to hit each other. Many of our children think that is the only way we can make each other do what we want.

College can make a child smart. You send your son or daughter to school; they will come back able to read and write and excel in classes. That is what schools are supposed to do, work with their minds. But the children's parents must make them wise.

We have some of the smartest young fools in the world. That is the truth. A lot of children today who are just outright smart can be downright stupid. You know why? They did not draw enough wisdom from their parents to be wise. Thus children know how to do everything in life but live skillfully. There must be in every home an environment in which hearts are more evident than heads and feelings are stronger than attitudes, so that wisdom can be taught by a wise parent.

Jamie, an upper middle class African American professional woman, said to me the other day, "We have a television in every room and I just never thought of the fact that our daughter never came out of her room to be with or talk to me and her dad. She always stayed in her room. She would come straight home from school, go to her room, come out and eat, and go back in her room. Sometimes she would eat in her room. We just didn't see her a lot."

It is amazing that parents live in the same house with their children and never talk to them. They do not eat together, play together, or pray together. This mother and her daughter stayed in the same house and never talked. It never occurred to that mother to go in and get rid of the television. The reason Jamie was talking with me was because she had discovered that somebody had stolen her daughter's heart. She wanted it back. She came to me, but she would have gone to anybody, and said, "Can I have my daughter's heart back?"

Most parents do not know what their children believe any more. They do not have time to ask them. When they do ask, the child answers so fast it is not possible to catch their words and the parents never look at their eyes and see that they are lying with what they are saying.

In Proverbs 4:23, the father says to his son, "Watch over your heart, son." Notice it carefully, for it says do it diligently "for from it flow the springs of life." The heart in this text is perceived to be the central organ that is in every human being. The heart of a man controls all of a man's feelings, his thinking, and his activities. As is a man's heart, so will be his character. As is the child's heart, so will be their character. The verse says that out of the heart flows the springs of life. You see, the heart of a child dictates what that child says.

The heart also controls what children focus on with their lives. The heart determines the path children take in life and it is the glue that binds those children to their goals. "Watch over your heart with all diligence, for from it flow the springs of life." Notice verse 24, "Put away from you a deceitful mouth." The heart dictates what you say. "Put away from you a deceitful mouth" and "Let your eyes . . ." The heart determines what you will focus on. "Let your eyes look directly ahead" (v. 25). That is what you focus on. Look at verse 26, "Watch the path of your feet." The heart determines your behavior. Look at verse 27, "Do not turn to the right." No wonder the verse says, "Watch your heart . . ." That is where a person's character is settled.

When you listen to what your children talk about to you, you are listening to their heart. That is why you need to listen to your child. When you sit down and listen to the child's conversation you are looking into their heart. At my house you can get in serious trouble when you stop talking to the rest of us. I will say to my children, how come it is that I am feeding you every day and I do not deserve at least a "Hello, daddy. And how was your day?"

When you watch what your children do socially and for entertainment, you are watching the heart. Children who scream at their sisters and brothers will show you that they are growing mean in their hearts. When you observe the direction your child is moving educationally, morally, and ethically, you are looking at his or her heart. They do what they are. It is hard for parents who have children who lie and steal to accept the fact that their children have become liars and thieves.

The African American parent will say without apology in defense of their kids, "Not my kid. Not ever." The reality is many parents are in denial as it pertains to the kind of heart that is developing in their children. Hard words, but it is true.

I said to one of my classes at Dallas Seminary "If you think I preach hard, read Peter's sermon in Acts 2. He was harder than I am." My words might be harsh but they are not wrong. I am simply raising the issue of at what point did the child become what he or she is? What is your boy? A pimp? A hustler? A good boy on his way somewhere? When do we finally say, "You know, son, you are a thief. You stole a car?" "They should not have left the keys in it," the kid will say. "Anybody could have stolen that car."

Parents must believe that what they are looking at in the behavior of the child is in fact an expression of the developing character. I believe my children can turn out bad. I work at trying to keep that from happening. I do not think that my children are going to inherit my commitment to Jesus Christ. It is not theologically accurate to say that they are born into the faith because they are mine.

My children are born sinners, They have become saved sinners. They are not going to evidence any behavior that suggests that they inherited some of my commitment to Christ. They must develop their own level of spiritual commitment. This is the case with all children. It really bothers me for somebody to say "And her daddy's a preacher too." So what? Does that means that child is less of a sinner? Not in my house.

Teach your children how to guard their hearts and they will know how to live well. When I say to you that forty-two percent of all murders in this country are committed by blacks against blacks, I am talking about young people with bad hearts and bad character.

When I say to you that today we are eleven percent of the population and represent some fifteen to twenty-five percent of the AIDS virus, I am telling you that we have heart problems and character problems. When I say to you this day that nearly half of African American babies born in this country are born out of wedlock, I am telling you that we have character problems. That is what we have. We do face serious social, economic, legal, and domestic problems but the evidence keeps on confirming that in black America we have some character problems that we must address in the home as African American parents.

A Call to Action: Parents to the Rescue

Parents must wake up and acknowledge to themselves that they are raising bad children. In reality the only other alternative is to remain in denial until the police lock our children up. Every parent has the responsibility of managing their child no matter how big he may be or whatever she might be. To be a parent is to be in charge of the children. Mothers and fathers in the church are increasingly at odds over their children and it is not unusual to find the mother wrong and the father right about their boy, because African American mothers make serious errors in overprotecting their sons from their fathers. Every son needs to be disciplined by his father.

There are a number of good people. We must never forget that those forty to sixty percent of black inmates in prisons and jails around this country are most often in prison because they raped, killed, maimed, and stole from other black people. These offenses were not committed by blacks in the white community against white people, which is just as evil, but these crimes most often happened in our own community. We are the victims of our own poor parenting.

It is no less disheartening to me when the person who breaks into my car and steals from me is African American. The fact is, I have been violated. As African American parents we must take charge of our children and act the part of parents. This means being a model before the children of godly character wrapped in transparent integrity.

There is no group, agency, organization, or institution designed by God to take the place of parents. Thus people who decide to make a baby must undertake the responsibility of raising that child into a healthy adult. It does not matter whether the parents remain married, nor does it really count if the child is born out of wedlock. The fact is it is the responsibility of the parents to raise the child into an adult.

PART 2

TELLING IT LIKE IT IS

CHAPTER 5

PROBLEMS FACED BY AFRICAN AMERICAN PARENTS

In addressing the issue of "The African American Christian Parent: Parenting in a Spiritual Deficit," I do not mean to imply that the uniqueness of African American parenting is such that African American parents do not share anything in common with non-African American parents. The fact is, in many ways parenting is the same across different races. Yet in those instances where there are differences, those differences really do matter.

There are at least seven areas in which the African American parent faces problems in the parenting process. These are (1) Time to parent; (2) Inadequate income; (3) Too few positive role models; (4) Non-Christian extended family; (5) Negative environment in the home and community; (6) Peer pressure; and (7) Negative communication.

First, they are challenged with having the time to parent. The most commonly perceived struggle parents face is economic. The fact that the highest number of poor people in this country are children of single black parents gives credence to this idea. Today's social workers appear to believe that the extent to which a parent is able to provide for his or her child determines the success of the child.

While all credit must be given to the benefits inherent in parenting when there is adequate income, inadequate income is just one of the major problems many black parents face. The African American parent today is so driven by the desire to attain a middle-class standard of living or to just survive economically that, in many instances, they have far too little time to parent their children.

Increasingly mothers today are given less than twenty-four hours in the hospital for the delivery of their children. They have only a few days off work before they must return to the job. The baby is in daycare before reaching the age of six weeks. The baby spends eight to ten hours in daycare, five days a week, leaving the mother less than two hours a day to be with the child and even less time to be with the baby's father. In this sense, time to parent is the missing ingredient.

Couples must determine that time with their children is just as important as is their standard of living. It is the absence of time with the children that has given rise to the prevalence of gangs in our community. Gangs are nothing more than surrogate parents headed by youths who are bonded together to fill a void in their lives left by their working and too busy parents.

In too many instances parents think that it is possible to parent part-time and produce healthy adults. Such is not the case. Parents who want to grow healthy adults must decide to invest the time necessary to raise them that way. This might mean lowering the standard of living. On the other hand, single mothers must find a way of banding together with other single parents and combining their resources so that they can all afford to spend more time with their children. This means being willing to sacrifice more of their personal time to spend time with their children.

In my community of Dallas, Texas, it is not just the children of poor parents who are in trouble and belonging to gangs. Children of middle and upper-class parents are equally represented among gangs. While the middle-class black parent and the poor black parent differ economically, they both are paupers in terms of time available to spend parenting their children.

My generation grew up in a society where our mothers spent time parenting the children of white people for whom they worked as maids. This time with other's children left those mothers too little time to mother their own children. Today black mothers spend their time striving to make ends meet economically, which in turn leaves them too little time to mother their children. The solution may just have to be a change in priorities.

The second major challenge African American parents face is inadequate income. Some groups are more likely to experience poverty than others. For instance, blacks are three times as likely to be poor as whites. Families headed by women are nearly five times more likely to be poor than other families. Families where the head of the house has no more than eight years of schooling are nearly five times as likely to be poor compared to families headed by a college-educated person.

Two of five persons classified as poor in 1988 were children under 18 years of age. This fact is of special social concern because poor children who are denied opportunities from the start are unfairly hindered in preparing themselves for productive adult lives later.

Low-income families are often driven into poverty by the birth of additional children. In 1988, 48.2 percent of families with five or more children lived in poverty, compared with 14.1 percent of two-children families. In a society that ignores the need for minimum wage laws and that balks at providing childcare for women so that they might earn needed income, a higher incidence of poverty among larger families is a logical consequence.

Poor children also have special needs beyond those which can be provided by giving their families higher incomes. In particular, health care, compensatory education, and vocational training are essential in providing permanent freedom from poverty.

The converse of this situation is unemployed and underemployed black men. The facts tend to show that a man who cannot financially support his children will abandon them to the welfare system, believing that they will fare better on public assistance than they would with an unemployed or underemployed father around.

The African American parent faces the financial challenge of parenting in an economic context in which, at best, they earn 76 cents to every dollar their white male counterpart earns. At worst, the African American parent must parent with income well below the national poverty line. Thus their children are often without the financial support to pursue higher education and, in many instances, have been pushed prematurely into the labor market in order to increase the family income.

The shortage of adequate income also contributes to the appeal of the illegal economy in the inner cities in that it provides access to money in large quantities with little effort. Facing the challenge of inadequate income means being willing to set attainable financial goals. It means learning contentment and being willing to sacrifice some things in order to provide greater opportunity for children, especially in the area of education.

The third major challenge parents face is that there are too few positive role models in the community. Published statistics show that the United States has the highest divorce rate in the world. In recent decades this rate has held fairly steady. In 1975 the rate was 4.9 per 1,000 people (over twice that of England and Wales) and in 1990 it was 4.7. In the United States, for every four marriages a divorce occurs. Divorce statistics, however, tend to be misleading. In 1990 about 2.4 million marriages took place in the United States and about 1.2 million divorces; thus one divorce occurred for every two marriages. It would be equally true, however, to say that 80 percent of all married people were still in their first marriage.

God's ideal family model as set forth in the Bible is what is commonly referred to as the nuclear family. The nuclear family is a family that consists of a man, his wife, and their children. There is little dispute about the fact that there are far too few family models like this in the black community. This shortage of models is a problem for the African American parent in that it often gives the impression that marriage is a temporary arrangement to be abandoned if it doesn't work out.

As parents, my wife and I find ourselves constantly reminding our children that marriage is an honorable God-ordained institution that must be honored by all Christians. The problem we face many times, however, is that the people who are the poorest examples of what God ordained marriage to be are fellow Christians.

In many instances the African American Christian parents who are models of the nuclear family are exceptions to the norm in the church, community, and in their own extended families. This shortage challenges these families to be more vocal about God's ideal family unit.

PROBLEMS FACED BY AFRICAN AMERICAN PARENTS

A few years ago, one of my son's teachers called our home regarding some problem he was having at school. I answered the phone and identified myself as my son's father. To my surprise the teacher questioned the legitimacy of my claim to be the father of my son. For whatever reason this teacher obviously was of the opinion that most black children do not live with both their own mother and father. There is indeed a serious shortage of positive models of the nuclear family in the black community.

Managing this shortage is a task that the black church should be involved in. The goal of the church should be to produce more positive role models of God's ideal for the family. This can be done by creating an ongoing ministry to families with a view to improving the quality of family life within the church.

The fourth challenge faced by parent is the presence of the non-Christian extended family. Unfortunately, much of the parenting done by African Americans today is done in the context of spiritual bankruptcy. This is where that which is spiritual is no longer relevant in the value system of people. I am not making the point that black people are not religiously inclined. They most certainly are and they have a history of religious involvement to prove it. However, today the black community is suffering from an absence of genuine biblically-based Christianity that is Bible-centered.

In many African American families the aunts, uncles, cousins, and sometimes grandparents are the most serious threat to Christian parents being able to indoctrinate their children with biblical Christianity. Most children find it difficult to accept the Christian world view of their parents when it can seldom seem to produce the same quality results as does the non-Christian world view of their extended family.

Children who live in a world where cheating leads to success and honesty leads to failure will find it difficult to embrace honesty. To some children the "wicked wing" of the family has more fun than they do. Thus the extended family which is a functioning part of the black family is a problem for the African American family.

The African American parent will want to make a clear distinction between the good religious people in their extended family and the Christian people in their extended family. Those who are permitted to share in the parenting of the children of Christian parents should share their Christian convictions.

The fifth challenge faced by African American parent is the negative environment that is frequently present in both home and community. In recent months much has been in the media about the environment in which black men like Mike Tyson and O. J. Simpson grew up. The prevailing opinion is that the negative environment in which these men found themselves contributed significantly to the crimes allegedly committed by these men.

There is little doubt about the fact that the environment in which children grow up contributes much to the shaping of their attitude, values, and general world view. Thus the African American parent must be concerned about the environment in which their children are being raised. For many African American children violence, death, brutality, abuse, and a host of other negative factors are a part of the environment in which they live every day of their lives. One cannot help but wonder what kind of adults these children will become.

In view of the frequently negative environment in the community combined with the negative stereotypical images of black people in the media and entertainment industry, the African American parent must strive to develop and maintain a positive environment in the home. This means, among other things, managing conflict in the home so that it does not poison the relationships in the family. This means learning how to communicate positively on a consistent basis and then maintaining open communication among the family members.

The sixth challenge is dealing with peer pressure. This is perhaps the most difficult problem most parents face in parenting. The difficulty is in the fact that most parents do not understand what peer pressure is and why it is such a strong influence in the life of their children.

Most parents believe that their child is so much like them that it is not possible for anyone of their child's age to be able to persuade them to do something that is contrary to what they have been taught. The fact is, however, that peer pressure is very real and very persuasive.

Peer pressure is the ability of children of the same generation to persuade each other to conform to a value system, lifestyle, and even criminal activity that is contrary to their own personal values, lifestyle, and integrity. The key element in peer pressure is the need that every child has to fit in and be accepted by their peers. This is really no different from their parents who also are given to conformity for the sake of acceptance.

The last challenge parents face is negative communication. The problem of communication is of monumental importance in that more than a few parents do not have the time to communicate with their children. Parents often lose touch with what their children are thinking and are therefore unable to communicate with them in any positive conversation.

The key to effective parenting is frequent, open, positive communication between parents and children. Parents must refuse to become merely critics of their children but must choose to be good listeners and a responders.

CHAPTER 6

RAISING A CHILD IN A VIOLENT SOCIETY

Like her mother, Sharon gave birth to her first child when she was sixteen years old. Also like her mother, Sharon's pregnancy ended her school days and she became another single African American teenage mother dependent upon public assistance for survival.

At age eighteen Sharon got involved with a man who was himself a high school dropout and a heavy drug user. This young man also had a violent temper and in time began to physically abuse Sharon. On the advice of her parents Sharon decided to end the relationship with him with a view to starting fresh and making something of her life. Sharon informed the young man that she would not see him again and he left. Sharon thought that he had accepted her decision and the relationship was over. After a few days the young man returned to Sharon's apartment and with the promise of just wanting to talk briefly she invited him in. A few minutes later shots rang out and Sharon and the young man were both found dead, lying in their own blood. The story as told by Sharon's brother is that this young man had informed his friends that he was going to kill Sharon, her son, and then himself. Unfortunately he succeeded in killing Sharon and himself. Fortunately he did not kill the three-year-old son.

As Sharon's pastor, I performed the funeral and I did my best to comfort her mother and father whom I had pastored for many years. When we arrived at the cemetery for the internment of Sharon's body, I was suddenly struck by the number of funerals that were occurring that day. I counted fourteen burials at that cemetery just during the time I was there. I checked to see who the people were who were being buried and, to my sorrow, I found out that ninety percent of the fourteen funerals I saw were African American men under the age of twenty-five.

It was this experience that shocked me into the realization that ours is a violent society. Our community is choking on the stench of blood shed by our own people. African American parents must raise their children in the context of a violent society.

Craig was sixteen years old and as I watched him over a period of a few weeks, I realized that he was seriously involved in drug dealing. Craig seemed to mock young men who worked for a living. He thought the real money was in dealing drugs. On one occasion Craig offered to finance the ministry of a young minister in the community from his drug money. Fortunately the young minister said no.

As the months passed Craig's visibility in the drug market seemed to grow. I remember remarking to a friend of mine that Craig would not live to see his twenty-first birthday. One Sunday morning, after Craig's grandmother had gone to church, Craig was killed. According to a family member who was home at the time, the phone rang and Craig was asked to meet someone in the apartment across the street. As Craig started across the street shots rang out from three different directions and he was killed. This was just a few months before his seventeenth birthday. The assassin literally blew Craig's brains out. All of the assassins were, like Craig, African American men.

Mr. Turner was the principal at an elementary school just around the block from the Institute for Black Family Renewal. One day Mr. Turner and one of his assistants decided to walk through the neighborhood and meet some of the parents. As they walked they came upon two young men with a gun. The young men robbed them, taking everything they had on them of value, even their shoes. However, what was most frightening was the repeated insistence of the younger of the two robbers that the older boy shoot Mr. Turner and his assistant. Fortunately, the older boy did not shoot them.

These examples are cited to focus on the violent nature of our society. It is my opinion that the most dangerous person in the African American community today is the young black male with a gun. It is commonly said that when a black person gets on an elevator with a white person, the white person will tighten the grip on his or her briefcase or purse. I have concluded that this action is not very different from the reaction of African American people to the young black males of today.

Raising a child in a violent society is a challenge of major proportions for every parent no matter where they live. Thus the nature of our times demands of every parent that serious consideration be given to how to parent in a violent society.

The first principle involved in raising a child in a violent society is *"Parents must anticipate the dangers and think through the possibilities."* As the father of two grown daughters and an eighteen-year-old son I have concluded that there are real dangers that must be thought through in dealing with this violence. These dangers include: physical violence, drug addition, criminal activity, sexual abuse, and peer pressure. Physical violence is an inner community danger for African American children and youth today. This is unlike the threat of violence faced by my generation in the forties and fifties.

Today African American parents must understand that their sons and their daughters are exposed to serious danger within the community. This danger comes from two primary sources. The first is from the peers of our children. In the community today, whether at school or on the streets, black youths are inclined to rob and kill each other with little provocation. To manage this danger our children must learn not to wear certain things in some contexts. They must also be willing to give up their possessions rather than risk their lives to keep them. But this is the easy part. What is more difficult is accepting the fact that violence is a common daily practice among a number of our own children.

It was much easier for my generation to avoid the rage of the white man in the south—we were taught to avoid him altogether. This was easy since we lived in separate communities. But this is not true today. The threat of violence is now black like my child and lives in my community. Avoiding violence for black children is a real challenge. Parents need to know this and act accordingly.

Another danger faced by African American children today is exposure to drugs. Parents must understand that the temptation to do drugs or become involved in drug trafficking most often comes from their friends and even relatives. Parents must watch their child's attitude, friends, social life, and habits. Learn to ask who their friends are, where they are going, and when they will return. Make sure you know where they are getting their money. Learn to take swift and decisive action when there is even the slightest hint of drug use with your child.

Closely related to drugs is the danger of involvement in criminal activity. Parents must understand that for an African American male to run up against the law is to get entangled in the judicial system. Parents must do everything possible to keep their children out of trouble with the law.

The fourth primary danger faced by black children is sexual abuse. This danger is primarily an exposure faced by black girls but not to the exclusion of black boys. The source of this danger is in the community and sometimes in the family. Thus parents must be careful with whom they entrust their children.

The fifth and final primary danger is peer pressure. This is the pressure young people place on each other to encourage them to conform to their agenda or principles. Choosing not to conform most often means being excluded from the group and/or physical abuse by the pressuring group. Most parents will probably have to accept some conformity on the part of their children with a good bit of tolerance. Yet parents must insist that the morals and values of the family be respected by the child.

Having identified the primary dangers that their children will face in growing up in a violent society, parents must think through the possibilities of how to parent in such a dangerous context. The goal in parenting is not only to avoid being killed or maimed for life. This is certainly important but the child must be kept from being damaged emotionally by society. This leads to the second principle in parenting in a violent context.

The second principle in raising a child in a violent society is "*Parents must equip the child to be alert to danger at all times."* Equipping a child to be alert at all times means teaching children to (1) think for themselves and not to entrust themselves to others, (2) always be on guard against certain dangers, and (3) not develop a false sense of security in the neighborhood and among their peers.

Much is said today about black life in "the hood." From the rhetoric that is spoken in the media and in the movies, one would conclude that "the hood" is a safe haven for black youths. If we are to believe the message of the nation of Islam, the major threat to black people in general and black men in particular are white people. While there was a time when this was certainly the case, I don't believe it is today. I know that all too well from the multitude of funerals I have both performed and attended of young black men who were murdered. These young black men were not murdered by white people—in fact most had not even been exposed to white people in any direct way. They were killed by black men.

African American parents today face the difficult task of equipping their children with the kind of wisdom that enables them to think for themselves and not entrust themselves to other people.

It was much easier for my parents to teach me not to entrust myself to white people because the community where I lived was all black and white people were viewed as outsiders who were not to be trusted. White people could walk all over a black neighborhood without any fear of anybody. Black people, however, could not walk around in the white community without risk of being stopped, harassed, beaten, or sometimes even killed. However in this day of vanishing black men, it is the black male who is pulling the trigger and killing his own race in his own neighborhood. Thus black parents must identify a potential life-threatening enemy as the residents of their own neighborhood. The sons and daughter of black parents have a new adversary with whom they must contend. That new adversary is sometimes the child next door.

Wilbert was a handsome young man, well-mannered and hard-working. His mother worked hard as a single parent to provide him with the best she could afford. To her delight, Wilbert graduated from high school and went on to college. As a college student, Wilbert did well and became a member of one of the campus fraternities. A few months into the school year, that fraternity gave a party and, as usual, Wilbert decided to go. For reasons known only to the young men involved in the incident, Wilbert was shot to death by one of the young men that attended the party.

This incident shows that, contrary to what many parents may think, violence among young black youths is not confined to the inner city. The violence that is plaguing our community seems to be inherent in the general attitude of young men today, regardless of where they are.

It is in the context of violence that African Americans must parent their children. Thus it is essential that they equip their children with the kind of survival skills that empower them to anticipate the potential of violence so they can learn how to survive it or avoid it altogether.

Parents must help their children see the community as the war zone that it often is. Parents cannot give their children a false sense of security about the community. Just because the people who reside there are black does not mean that it is safe to be there. This is a new kind of attitude that must be developed in African American parents and passed on to their children. There are some places in the community that children must be warned to stay away from. Children must also be taught to watch out for themselves and learn how to sense danger and flee.

In Fort Worth, Texas, a seventeen-year-old African American was sentenced to life in prison for killing a young man and his girlfriend in order to steal the sound system in the man's car. The couple that was killed happened to be riding through the neighborhood listening to music. The man who killed them heard the sound system and recognized the quality of the sound. He then told his friends that he had to have that sound system. His parting comment as he walked away with what he wanted was that when he shot the young man, he fell like a rag doll.

I must hasten to add that not all of the black community fits the profile of being violent. There is, however, a prevailing propensity towards violence that is increasingly prevalent in the black community.

The third principle involved in growing a child in a violent society is *"Parents need to provide a strong family structure."* It is unfortunate today that the majority of black children are being born into and growing up in single parent families. While many single parents are doing a great job with their children, single parenting is not God's ideal in parenting. The basic structure of a parenting family requires the presence of a man who fathers his own children.

The structure of the family provides the context in which a child gets a number of necessary things such as love and protection. However in terms of raising a child in a violent society, the family structure is the source from which the child obtains the necessary wisdom to live. The primary source of that wisdom is the parents.

Having heard my lecture on family structure, one of my students understood me to have said that single parents are contributing to the growing number of delinquent children, especially among black boys. This student was herself a single parent with a daughter whom she had parented well. She said to me, "Professor, it seems to me that single parents today are blamed for most of the ills affecting the African American family." Then she added, "You seem to be contributing to this ridiculous notion."

In response to this student, I said my emphasis on family structure in which I highlighted the necessity of two parents to have a structure within which children can grow into healthy adults is not intended to criticize, judge, condemn, or cast dispersion on single parents. For indeed, many single parents produce healthy, strong adults. My point is that a single parent family is a family with a weak structure. The single parent is like a bridge that is half of what it must be to function as it is designed to function. To acknowledge that the single parent family is a weak structure is to suggest that ways must be sought and found to strengthen that structure.

This student contracted with me to do an independent study in which she set out to prove that single parenting was not essentially weaker than two parent families. At the end of the study, she had proven that single parents, while a genuine family structure, is indeed best described as weak and thus in need of both internal and external support. It seems evident to me that in spite of the prevalence of single parent families in the African American community, we must steadfastly contend that a two parent family is the most secure structure in which to raise a child as a healthy adult.

It is within the family structure that the fourth principle is applied and that is *"Growing children in a violent society means teaching the child a high respect for authority."* Respect for authority is a protective shield against such things as police brutality, involvement in drugs, and criminal activity. It is a recognized fact that the greater number of young blacks who are in prison today grew up in a weak family structure where respect for authority was low or nonexistent. It is equally true that a large portion of the unwed mothers in our community grew up in a weak family structure with little regard for authority.

Respect for authority is key in obtaining an education and developing positive relationships. It is also an essential ingredient in parenting. A weak family structure tends to expose the child to a myriad of dangers including an absence of recognized limitations.

Like most people today, I have grown accustomed to the unimaginable things people say about themselves and their friends and family on television talk shows. However, I was shocked and angered when I saw a mother and her son on a show during which the mother said she was literally afraid of her own son. I could not help but think that had that boy been the son of my mother, he would have been afraid of her no matter how big he was!

It is my contention that respect for authority is essential to proper family structure. Children must not be considered as having been parented properly when they have no respect for authority.

The fifth principle in growing a child in a violent society is *"Teach your children how to manage anger and provocation."* My wife and I have three children, all of whom are six years apart. As our children were growing up there was never a time when they were allowed to express their anger in physical violence toward each other. Our home was not a place where this was permitted at anytime by anybody. Our children also never saw any form of violence in our home.

I finished high school without ever having a single fight with anybody. Physical violence was not a part of my philosophy in either expressing anger or in responding to provocation. Because of our attitude towards violence my wife and I concluded that our children would all adopt the same attitude toward violence that we did. Our two daughters did just that. However our son, who is the youngest of the three, did not adopt this attitude. He would fight when he was angry and provoked.

Our son is now eighteen, and although he has made significant improvement in managing his anger, he will still fight, especially when he is provoked. In teaching our son how to manage anger and respond properly to provocation, it was necessary for us to discover the source of his anger. We knew the source was not in the home environment. We discovered that much of our son's anger was rooted in the prejudice and discrimination he experienced in kindergarten in a white private school. Once we discovered this, we were able to help him overcome the feelings of rage that overcame him due to the abuse he sometimes experienced in this private school.

In teaching a child to manage anger and provocation, it is always necessary for the parent to determine whether or not the child is already angry about something in their past experience or whether there is something in the immediate situation that is causing the anger. Once that determination is made the parent can begin to help the child manage the anger.

Managing anger means learning to deal with anger in a constructive rather that a destructive way. This means having the discipline to listen, think, talk about, and understand the situation. Managing provocation means learning to respond rather than react to what is said or done. In the area of anger and provocation some good parents, in an attempt to get for their child a good Christian education, make the mistake of disregarding the negative effects of racial prejudice upon the attitude of their child. Thus the child becomes angry and bitter at an early age.

Lest I be misunderstood in speaking of our experience with the exclusive white private school, I will speak of a specific situation. His teachers (who were all white) would put a big red "F" on his paper when he did not do well. They would not put anything on his paper when he did well. My wife and I asked a few of the white parents about how their children were graded, and, according to these white parents, the teachers never put an "F" on their children's paper for fear of damaging their self-esteem. It seemed to us that these teachers did not have the same concern for the self-esteem of our son as they did for the white children.

This is just one of many hurdles we faced in trying to get for our son an education in a white evangelical Christian school. For us this was a bad parenting choice.

The sixth principle in growing a child in a violent society is *"Teach your children how to manage conflict."* Conflict is not something that can be avoided so the goal must be to learn how to manage it in such a way that it is not destructive.

Parents must teach their children how to prioritize the individual so that the issue and not the individual becomes the focus. Managing conflict means setting boundaries for the argument which do not permit attacking the individual. In managing conflict, children need to be taught that physical violence is not an option.

Essential to developing the ability to manage conflict is the skill of verbally communicating effectively combined with the discipline to be quiet and even walk away as an alternative to destructive behavior. However, I was recently introduced to a new way of managing conflict by my son. The method could be described a conflict avoidance. According to my son, one of the better ways of avoiding conflict is knowing how to look, walk, and talk in a manner that indicates that you are not intimidated by what's happening around you. This method of conflict avoidance is called "mean mugging." The objective is to stare down someone else so it is apparent to all that you are not intimidated. This behavior is not unlike the behavior I have observed in the wild when a lion finds himself in the territory of another herd of lions. Lions are good at "mean mugging" other lions.

The seventh principle in raising a child in a violent society is *"Be a positive mentor for your child."* In a society where the most visible examples of high living are the members of the drug economy and when drive-by shootings are a daily experience, it is difficult for parents to grow children who do not adopt a violent way of life. The challenge that parents face is in providing an alternative model where that which is positive is demonstrated to be the most successful path of life.

Negative parents will undoubtedly grow negative children. Parent who fight will most often grow children who fight. A violent society produces violent children. These things being true, parents must become vocal and visible models of alternatives to violence. This means that parents do more than say what is right; they demonstrate it on a consistent basis.

The eighth principle in parenting in a violent society is *"Equip your child with high moral standards."* Parents must realize that, in addition to the dangers faced by their children from physical violence at the hands of their peers, there is the ever-present threat of AIDS. The threat of contracting the AIDS virus is equal to physical violence in terms of dangers faced by our children.

The most effective protection against the AIDS virus is not safe sex but rather high moral standards. High moral standards means abstaining from sexual immorality and limiting all sexual activity to the context of marriage. It is teaching the child how to manage his/her body with sanctification and honor.

The ninth and final principle involved in growing a child in a violent society is *"Teach your child respect for life."* Children who have a high appreciation for life are children that will endeavor to protect their own lives. Such a child will have a vision for their future and thus will be less inclined to risk their life or to take someone else's life.

Mark's son finally broke the news to his parents that he had impregnated his girlfriend and he was going to drop out of high school and get a job so he could marry his girlfriend and take care of his family. Much to Mark's surprise, his parents responded with a tremendous amount of anger to his solution, insisting that he get the idea of quitting school and getting married out of his head. When things quieted down, Mark asked his parents what their idea was as an alternative plan that would enable him to take care of his child as they had taken care of him. Without hesitation Mark's parents told him that his girlfriend should get an abortion and both of them should go on and complete their education. His parents seemed not to be aware of the fact that they had demonstrated to their son a serious disregard for human life.

The idea of being pro-life is a principle that children must learn from the example of their parents. Parents for whom abortion is an option may well be teaching something less than a high priority for life.

Chapter 7

Educating a Child in a Racist Society

Racism refers to any theory or doctrine stating that inherited physical characteristics, such as skin color, facial features, or hair texture determine behavior patterns, personality traits, or intellectual abilities. In practice, racism typically takes the form of a claim that some human "races" are superior to others. An abuse of the concept of differences among peoples, it has contributed to prejudice and discrimination among groups in many parts of the world.

The causes of racism are complex and cannot be reduced to a single factor. It's rise and fall are often linked to conflicts of interest and competition for scarce resources. Historically racism has accompanied slavery, colonialism, and other forms of exploitation and inequality. In other cases powerless groups that have felt threatened by social and economic instability have blamed other powerless groups for their predicament. The insecure white working class and lower middle class of industrial societies have often expressed racist attitudes toward defenseless minorities, such as blacks in the United States or Commonwealth immigrants in Great Britain.

Discrimination in a society can be defined as the unequal treatment of equals. Another way of putting it is to say that a person is denied equal opportunity for reasons that are not relevant to the task at hand. Discrimination may be experienced by ethnic minorities—with the term ethnic encompassing race and religion as well as national and cultural traditions. Occasionally, as in South Africa, the majority group is the target of discrimination. Discrimination may also be directed at women, the elderly, handicapped people, and homosexuals, to name just a few.

One of the most challenging experiences faced by African American believers is the ever-present reality of racism in the Christian community. The Christian church is not only the most segregated institution in this country on Sunday morning, but the Christians who are the members of these segregated churches are often among the most racist people in the marketplace.

As an African American parent and pastor, I wish I could include in this section a positive summary of the difference that Christianity makes in a racist society. Unfortunately this is not possible. Although I have many friends who are white and I have met a number of white people who do not embrace racist attitudes, stereotypes, and action, in actuality these men and women tend to be the exception, rather than the rule.

The great challenge we face today as Christians is to work towards reconciliation between the different races that make up the church. Today both white and black parents are growing children who tend to be nationalistic in their world view. This nationalism tends to produce people who are more committed to their race and culture and the divisiveness inherent in that kind of world view than to the commitment of the inherent unity all believers share in the body of Christ. The challenge we face as believers is to change this kind of attitude.

In the society in which I grew up, black people were viewed by white people as something less than human. The idea of separate but equal was the umbrella under which whites and blacks lived, with only some degree of harmony between them. In that society, segregation was so strictly enforced and violations of Jim Crow laws were so violently punished that few black people ever ventured beyond the boundaries of their racial limitations, either socially, economically, educationally, or politically. To be white in that society was to feel entitled to life without any limitations. It was considered the birthright of white people to be privileged because of the color of their skin.

Survival was the name of the game for children born in that context. The goal for black parents was to grow their children with the kind of high regard for the superiority of all whites, men, women and children, that caused them to both fear, respect, and also avoid offending them. It was the opinion of my parents that if I could survive the racial prejudice of whites in East Carol parish, then I had a chance of growing up and getting out of that oppressive environment. I am among the few of those who were born into that racist context that made it out. My parents equipped me to survive.

My parents equipped me to survive the ever-present danger of violent white men against black boys. This principle of survival is illustrated in an incident that happened to me when I was seventeen years old. I was in the process of taking my girlfriend out when my car was hit by another driven by a seventeen-year-old white boy. There were two other passengers in the car that hit me—a young white girl and a white teenage boy. When things settled down and my girlfriend and I discovered that we had been hit by a car driven by white youths, we both became frightened. In fear she ran off and left me to face these two young white boys myself.

In that situation the survival skills my parents had taught me kicked in and immediately I knew I had to do two things. First, I had been taught never to face more than one white man in a confrontation by myself. This meant that I had to immediately find someone to stand with me out there on that country road with these two white boys. Within minutes I located my two buddies and they joined me. This meant that there was three of us and two of them now. We had been taught that white men usually attacked black men only when they were the greater number. It happened that as soon as these two boys discovered that there were three of us and only two of them they backed off and waited on the arrival of the police.

This brought to the surface the second survival principle I had been taught by my parents, namely when the white policeman arrived, quietly do whatever he tells you to do—and do not talk back to him. So when I attempted to explain to the police what happened and he ordered me to be quiet and to go sit down somewhere, that is exactly what I did. According to the report turned in by that policeman, everything the white boys said was truth and the accident was my fault. As an aside, that report was not something my father accepted. Through this incident, he taught me how to fight injustice even if you lose.

In the racist society in which I was raised, the name of the game for black parents was equipping their children for survival. Today the society in which black parents must parent is just as racist as the one in which I grew up. However, the name of the game is different. The name of the game today is equipping the child to compete and win in a racist society. I had to have the skill to encounter the white man in a racist context and survive that encounter, and now my children must have the skill to encounter whites in this racist society, compete with them, and win.

There is a major difference in the term "survival skills" and in the term "competitive skills." Most often surviving racism in my youth meant passively accepting whatever white people said or did to you as if it was their right to say it or do it. Competition, on the other hand, demands a proactive attitude. It demands meeting the racist on either equal or unequal turf and accepting the challenge and striving for the goal, holding nothing back.

As a parent who has raised two adult daughters and is in the process of raising a son, I have determined that there are some areas in which African American parents must equip their children to compete with white people. Theses areas of competition include but are not limited to the following: (1) academics on all levels, (2) the field of technology and health care, (3) sports, (4) upward mobility—professionally, economically, socially, and politically, (5) music, (6) business management, and (7) private enterprise (ownership of business).

Equipping a child to compete and win in a racist society means that parents must anticipate the kinds of institutionalized racist experiences their children will experience in various contexts. This equipping must have both a short-term and a long-term effect.

The African American parent must remember that in North America, race matters. Thus, parenting must be done in such a way that African American children are not defeated by the racist experiences that they will encounter in their lives. This experience begins in elementary school and continues into adulthood.

The African American parent must anticipate the racist experiences the child will, in most cases, experience in the public and private colleges and universities. Educational institutions in our country are highly successful in channeling black students into useless majors. My experience with trying to educate my children in a Christian private school proved to be a disaster in terms of the negative effect it had on my children. As a result, I am not an advocate of Christian academies. In my mind the public school system is a far better option. There are excellent teachers in the public school system who are born-again Christians and do a fine job of educating children.

However, in more than a few instances, especially in neighborhood where whites are the majority, both black and white teachers tend to evidence an attitude that says to the students that race matters. In this setting, racist attitudes show up in how a number of the teachers and administrators respond to students of different races. For instance, I have found that, in general, white students tend to be treated with far more understanding and support than black students in predominantly white schools. This is evident in the number of black students who are sent to the principal's office for disciplinary purposes as compared to white students, and also the number of black students placed in special education classes as compared to white students.

Teachers tend to help the white student succeed in their course work far more than they do black students. In fact, many black students contend that some teachers, black as well as white, will give the white student a better grade when their work indicates they deserve a lower grade, while at the same time giving the black student a lower grade when their work indicates they have earned a better grade.

In difficult subjects white students tend to be given real assistance in understanding the subject matter, while black students are quickly sent off to the resource center for help, only to discover that the staff there are really not interested in helping them. In those classes where the black student succeeds, the teachers tend to disregard the raised hand of the black student, choosing to focus on the white student who did not raise their hand.

The most supportive faculty person in the life of black

students on the public school and university campus are the sports coaches. However their interest is all to often limited to athletics, and they tend not to encourage and motivate black students to pursue academics.

In college the situation does not differ much from the public school system in terms of racist attitudes and behavior. The black student who chooses a field of concentration that is more difficult and will prove to be economically beneficial to the student when they graduate will find that not many blacks are actually in those fields of concentration. This low concentration of blacks in the more difficult fields of study puts the black student at a serious disadvantage since the white students will likely think that the black students are in that field as a matter of quota rather than intellect. The thinking often is that they have not earned the right to pursue a career in that field. At the same time the professors will tend not to give the black student any assistance. The white students will get together and pool their research in figuring out difficult answers but they will exclude the black student. In addition the advisor to the those students will give them bad and wrong academic counseling in order to dissuade them from continuing on in their chosen field.

As a child, my parents equipped me to survive racism in the area of academia. This meant learning how to learn with inadequate educational facilities and recourses. The African American parent today must equip their children to compete with white people in spite of racism and equip them to win. This means being tough enough to go it alone and make it without becoming embittered. In the racist context in which my generation grew up in the South, the legal script read, "separate and equal." The reality was instead though, "separate but unequal." This really meant as it pertained to education, "access denied."

I never saw a single African American doctor, lawyer, or nurse growing up. In my world of education there were only a few of my teachers who had more than a high school education. There were no chemistry teachers in my high school. There was only one math teacher and science was not something we practiced in a lab. The name of the game was "access denied" in terms of the education of black children in my community. My parents equipped me to survive that racist context and I did.

Today black children have access to any kind of education they want. At least that is what the civil rights legislation was all about. The trouble is that educational institutions have made racism an effective tool that kills off the spirit of the child so that they lose the will to compete in the academic arena, oftentimes before they reach their teens. This is especially true of black boys who have no resident father involved in their lives.

I have educated two children with a third child a senior in high school, and further, I have close to thirty years experience in pastoring parents with children who have encountered racism in education. I should also mention that I have spent more than twenty years on the campus of a predominantly white graduate school as an administrator and professor. What I have learned in all of this is that race matters and racism is alive and well in North American educational institutions today. The African American parent must equip their child to compete in the arena of academia in spite of the racism.

In thinking my way through this section on racism in education I asked my son how the black students who socialize with white students were treated on his high school campus. His response was quite interesting. He said, "They are treated better than other black students but not as good as whites." The point is that race matters and black parents must equip their child to compete in a racist society, while at the same time maintaining their own racial and cultural identity.

In raising children in a racist society, parents must finds ways of participating with the child in their racist experiences. These are not days in which the parent can assume that the teacher, police, store owner, or anyone who accuses their child of something is right and the child in wrong. For instance, a child who is failing a particular subject may in fact be the victim of racism. The parent must listen to the child. Parents cannot leave the resolution of conflict to the principal of the school—the parent must get involved in the situation and share the experience with the child.

Black parents know full well that in certain contexts being black means being excluded. To be black is to be perceived as something less than qualified. Thus the parent must provide love, companionship, and a positive social

Parenting in the Context of a Spiritual Deficit

context for the child. This kind of provision on the part of the parents will go a long way in keeping the spirit of the child alive. When children fail academically, parents must love them back to success. This means providing every possible assistance and motivation for the child.

Raising a child in a racist society means equipping a child to desire success in their field of concentration. This means training a child to think more of their success than the injustice they are experiencing. To accomplish this, parents must teach their child how to handle their frustration, rage, and anger.

I am of the opinion that there are more black children who abandon their professional goals because someone makes them angry and they quit, than there are those who flunk out because they lack the intellectual ability to compete. The student who learns to hate the teacher and despise the class will most often fail the course, quit the job, or abandon the position. Managing anger is key in competing in a racist society.

Men of my generation were known to lose control of their temper when they were called a "nigger" or a "boy" by a white man. This meant that at any time black men could be provoked to rage. Dick Gregory wrote a book called "Nigger" which went a long way towards equipping black people to deal with this kind of provocation.

The African American parent must understand that a racist society will with few exceptions destroy the self-esteem of their children. Self-esteem can be defined as the ability to feel good about oneself as a human being in relation to others no matter what their race or culture. Self-esteem is a thing of the spirit which propels an individual to a level of excellence and equality with others.

In America racism remains a primary tool used to destroy the self-esteem of black children. Thus parents must guard the self-esteem of their children. This means insisting that every individual who has access to the mind and spirit of the child highly regard the self-esteem of the child. Parents should not permit family, caregivers, teachers or any other person to treat the child as deficient in intellect, creativity, intelligence or appearance.

The parent must be willing to guard and defend the self-esteem of the child. This means being alert to "code words" that infer that to be black and different is to be intellectually inferior and poor. In addition to defending the self-esteem of the child the parent must also reinforce their self-esteem. This means doing and saying the kind of things that make children feel good about themselves.

Growing up in the rural south in the forties and fifties meant being called a "nigger" and being treated as such by white people. I understood that term to mean that because you are black, you were dirty, ignorant, immoral, lazy, dishonest, and a host of other undesirable adjectives. However, in my home these negative stereotypes were overruled by the constant reminders my parents gave me of how significant, handsome, and smart I was. In my home, I was the pride of my parents, thus it really did not matter what white people thought of me.

My parents reinforced my self-esteem in every way they knew how. My father made sure that my clothes were purchased at the most exclusive store in Lake Providence. This was the same store where the wealthy white men purchased their clothes. Our food came from the uptown grocery store where the white people shopped. You see, my parents wanted me and my brother and sisters to believe that we were as good as white people even though we were different from them.

Finally, raising a child in a racist society means educating the child with the kind of education that includes, but is not limited to, these areas. *First, their education must provide credentialing in marketable skills.* This means insisting that children get the kind of general education that will enable them to succeed in an academic or vocational context that grants degrees/certificates that are recognized in the marketplace. Parents must refuse to allow their children to enroll in programs that do not equip them with credentials or that only produce assistants to those who are credentialed. There are no small number of programs in all kinds of colleges and universities that are, at best, a waste of time and money. Most sons and daughters of African Americans will need more than just athletic abilities to make it as an adult. Parents must insist that they get more.

Second, their education will need to equip them with survival skills. This means exposing the child to the dangers inherent in the racist society in which they live. Learning how to survive means knowing how to recognize danger. It means being alert to risky situations, having a high regard for authority, and being willing to try harder with a strong work ethic for support.

Third, they must be equipped with a strong sense of self-worth. This means teaching a child to have a strong appreciation for their own body, their family, friends, and their reputation. It means teaching a child the value of life and good health.

Last, it must equip them with a strong personal self-identity. This means allowing the child to develop as an individual with his or her own unique strengths and weaknesses. Black children need to be proud of their family heritage and the traditions of their black forefathers.

Raising a child in a racist society means growing a child who is balanced and well-rounded emotionally, physically, and spiritually. It is developing a child who is able to function effectively in a society that is often unfair, cruel, and destructive.

CHAPTER 8

DOUBLE CONSCIOUSNESS: AN AFRICAN AMERICAN REALITY

For those of my generation who grew up in the south, the prevailing idea of culture was that there was only one culture and class that counted and both were white. We were taught that white culture was right and black culture was fit only for the black church and the black community. In the company of white people, our grammar, attitude, and behavior changed. We even dressed different when we were going to be among whites. In that case, clean underwear was a must, in case something happened and we had to go to the doctor, who was also white.

For blacks of my generation, the great American idea of a cultural melting pot was nothing more than a myth. The fact was, from our point of view, if there was such a thing as a cultural melting pot, we were not in that pot. The only cultural pot blacks saw was one that consisted of white culture and values. It was the goal of my generation to access that pot as much as possible given the handicap of the color of our skin.

It is in this setting that the concept of a double consciousness developed. On this subject, W. E. B. Du Bois, United States civil rights leader (1868–1963) said, "It is a peculiar sensation, this double-consciousness, this sense of always looking at one's self through the eyes of others, of measuring one's soul by the tape of a world that looks on in amused contempt and pity."[1]

This double consciousness of which Du Bois wrote is with us today in the experience of our children. One African American woman put it this way, "When I am with black clients I am just as professional as I am with white clients in terms of doing what I do. However with black clients I feel much freer to joke and tease about different things. I am less conscious about my grammar. With white clients I give a lot more attention to what I say and how I say it. I often get the feeling when I am with white clients that they are not real sure that I know what I am doing. This is not the case with blacks, they are proud to see a black person doing what I do." The experience of this young professional woman mirrors not only what Du Bois commented about a double consciousness but also what Jesse Jackson said about being black in America. "The burden of being black is that you have to be superior just to be equal. But the glory of it is that, once you achieve, you have achieved, indeed."[2]

In the society in which I grew up being able to acclimate to white culture was considered an asset in that it allowed one limited access to the white world. Thus as a student "talking black" was severely criticized by teachers. The reality was that my generation was raised in such a way that we were in conflict with our culture and thus we were in conflict with our race and who we were as a people. However, we were mostly unaware of this conflict.

Today African Americans are still in a culture conflict as it pertains to white and black culture and class. However there is a significant difference in the conflict. The difference is that a number of those in today's genera-

---

[1] W. E. B. Du Bois, *The Souls of Black Folk* (1903). *The Columbia Dictionary of Quotations* is licensed from Columbia University Press. Copyright © 1993 by Columbia University Press. All rights reserved. Caedmon recordings reproduced by arrangement with Harper Collins Publishers.

[2] Jesse Jackson, quoted in *Christian Science Monitor* (September 26, 1979). *The Columbia Dictionary of Quotations* is licensed from Columbia University Press. Copyright © 1993 by Columbia University Press. All rights reserved. Caedmon recordings reproduced by arrangement with Harper Collins Publishers.

tion of young people are heavily into black nationalism and have a genuine aversion to white culture. In the minds of a number of young black men and women the idea of dating a white person is unthinkable. It is considered to be a racial sell-out and a betrayal of the black race.

It is the high priority young African Americans place on their own race and culture in dress, attitude, values, and grammar combined with their rejection of white people and white culture and also the idea that whites are a people of privilege and have the culture of choice that puts the African American in conflict with white culture.

In this issue of young blacks being in conflict with white culture, the heart of the conflict resides in the fact that corporate America is structured to accommodate white culture. This structure demands of the modern day African American the same double consciousness that Du Bois spoke of in the early nineteen hundreds.

George Davis and Craig Watson, in their book *Black Life in Corporate America: Swimming in the Mainstream*, cite the statement of an elderly black woman that reflects the reality of the black/white cultural conflict. "Yes, we are all the same under God so we have the same problems, but colored folk have special ones, too. It's the same being colored as white but it's different being colored, too. It's the same, but it's different."[3] In my opinion, being black in America means knowing the truth of this statement from the distant past made by a old black woman. Blacks and whites are the same but they are different. It is the difference that is the root of the cultural conflict that results from being black in America.

Davis and Watson quote John T. Molloy, author of *Dress for Success*. "It is an undeniable fact that the typical upper-middle-class American looks white, Anglo-Saxon and Protestant. He is of medium build, fair complexion, with almost no pronounced physical characteristics. . . . Like it or not, his appearance will normally elicit a positive response from someone viewing him. Anyone not possessing his characteristics will elicit a negative response in some degree, regardless of whether that response

---

[3] George Davis and Craig Watson, *Black Life in Corporate America: Swimming in the Mainstream* (Garden City, NY: Doubleday Publishing Company, 1982), p. 22.

is conscious or subconscious."[4] It is this profile in corporate America of a person fitted for the corporate world that creates a conflict of culture in black men. In corporate America, the African American must dress and talk white even though he is black.

In his book *Race Matters*, West, gives this definition of Authentic Blackness: "Being black means being minimally subject to white supremacist abuse and being part of a rich culture and community that has struggled against such abuse."[5] In short, West says, "Blackness is a political and ethical construct."[6] West seems to be saying that authentic blackness is more related to the degree that an African American is subject to white supremacist abuse than it is related to the color of the skin.

In this definition of authentic blackness, West pinpoints a major problem African American parents face today in growing black children in white America. The problem is that, in general, black children are shielded from the struggle of oppression, political disenfranchisement, and discrimination by their parents. Thus black children grow up in a world where they develop a strong appreciation for black culture as is reflected in their dress, dance, grammar, and values, but to the degree the authenticity of their blackness is measured by their being subject to white supremacist abuse and thus their involvement in the struggle against such abuse, to that extent they are not really black. While it is true that all black people are potential victims of racism, it is not true that all black children are aware of the struggle against such an attitude.

Both of my daughters attended universities that are predominantly white. They were both, much to their surprise, the victims of serious prejudice and discrimination. Yet both were well into their twenties before either was called a "nigger" face to face by a white person. I can tell you that they were both seriously upset by this encounter. The fact is they were not emotionally prepared for such a frontal racist attack. Their mother and I had always shielded them from such experiences.

---

[4] Ibid., p. 83.

[5] Cornel West, *Race Matters* (Boston: Beacon Press, 1993).

[6] Ibid.

In his book, *The Coming Race Wars*, William Pannell quotes a missionary friend who said of the Los Angeles riots, "Those riots are not about race—it is all about culture."[7] Pannell disagrees with his friend's assessment of the cause of the Los Angeles riots, concluding that the real cause was power. It seems clear to me that the white and black struggle today is about both culture and power. The label may differ depending on the agenda that is being pursued, but the underlying issue is culture and power.

The African American parent, like parents of all races today, would do well to raise their children with the ability to appreciate and relate to people of any culture. While every race must retain their own culture in order to develop and maintain their own personal identity, they must also be able to relate to people of other cultures.

My wife and I decided to take our son abroad in 1994 in order to expose him to people of different cultures. It was interesting to observe that in London the whites we interacted with did not seem to know how to relate to us as people of color until they figured out our economic status. In London we discovered that our class was more important than our race. For our son the experience was invaluable as we visited London and the Middle East.

---

[7] William Pannell, *The Coming Race Wars: A Cry for Reconciliation* (Grand Rapids: Zondervan Publishing House).

CHAPTER 9

BLACK NATIONALISM AND ACCULTURATION

Culture, in anthropology, is the way of life of a human society, transmitted from one generation to the next by learning (of language and other symbolic media) and by experience. Cultural universals include social organization, religion, structure, economic organization, and material culture (tools, weapons, clothing). The spread of culture traits (customs, ideas, attitudes) among groups by direct or indirect contact is called diffusion. The general stages in cultural evolution are nomadic food gathering (as in the Old and Middle Stone Age); settled food producing (New Stone Age); and urban dwelling, as in all the great civilizations of the world.[1]

There are few ideas and attitudes with which the African American parent must contend that are more challenging than black nationalism. Black nationalism is perhaps the most prevailing contemporary social attitude adopted by black youth in general but, more specifically, among black boys. The *Grolier Encyclopedia* provides a brief historical perspective on Black Nationalism.

Black nationalism is the name given to revitalization movements among black Americans, emphasizing their African origins and identity, their pride in being black, their desire to control their own communities, and sometimes the desire to establish a black nation in Africa or some part of the

---
[1] *The Concise Columbia Encyclopedia* is licensed from Columbia University Press. Copyright © 1991 by Columbia University Press. All rights reserved.

United States. The exact origins of black nationalist movements are lost in the largely unwritten history of blacks in early America, but it is clear that such movements began as protests against the brutal and dehumanizing conditions of slavery. A few records indicate that early African protest against slavery conditions had overtones of black nationalism.[2]

The above historical perspective on black nationalism provides a basis from which to point out some of the value in black nationalism for parents. Black nationalism emphasizes the historical African roots of black Americans, hence the contemporary racial label "African Americans." Inherent in the idea of black nationalism is the personal self-identity of all black people as black African Americans. When people say they are black men or black American Christians, they are affirming their spirit of nationalism. The phrase, "I am black and I am proud" reflects a spirit of black nationalism. To be sure, no African American parent wants their child to grow up ashamed of the color of their skin or the texture of their hair, nor of their West African heritage.

At this point the value cited thus far for black nationalism is primarily personal in its benefit to African Americans. In addition to what has been cited, there are other aspects to black nationalism. These include the desire of blacks to control their own communities, and also the sometimes present desire to establish a black nation in Africa or in some part of the United States.

This dimension of black nationalism extends beyond the individual to the community. It includes the social, economic, and political dimensions of black people. While it is difficult to disagree with the notion of control over one's destiny, it is equally difficult to conclude that a separate black nation would be a utopia for black people any more than it is for the other one-race nations of the world.

The most visible example of the idea and the attitude of black nationalism today are the black Muslims, otherwise known as the Nation of Islam. Regarding the Muslims, the *Grolier Encyclopedia* notes,

> The Nation of Islam grew under the leadership of Elijah

---

[2] Copyright 1994 by Grolier Electronic Publishing, Inc.

Mohammed from the mid-1930s to the mid-1970s. Along with Islamic and Christian ideas it emphasized black pride, the central role of the male in the family, the importance of economic self-sufficiency, and a way of life that was often equated with middle-class morality. It exchanged the goal of a separate nation outside the United States for one of independence and autonomy within it. Perhaps its best-known leader was Malcolm X. An offshoot "Nation of Islam" led by Louis Farrakhan upholds these separatist ideas. By the late 1960s many themes of black nationalism had become part of the lifestyle of ordinary black Americans, particularly young people. These ideas persist today in colleges and universities, many of which have developed courses in black studies. [3]

The Nation of Islam has taken the idea of black nationalism to a higher plane in that it has added to its value both the priority of the role of the male in the family and the importance of economic self-sufficiency. It has maintained the historical idea of independence and autonomy of black people as a nation within the United States. In addition, the Nation of Islam has made black nationalism a popular part of the lifestyle of a significant number of black college and university students.

Laying aside for the moment the danger of black nationalism as it relates to parents raising Christian children, there are several dangers that are inherent in this ideology. These dangers are for the most part related to the social and political life of black people.

First, black nationalism, while valuable in many ways, tends to promise far more than it delivers in two primary areas of life. Black nationalism at both the local and national level tends to lack political power. There is little doubt about the fact that the Nation of Islam is more than just a little effective in attracting young black men. Today, thousands of black men embrace the nationalistic views inherent in black nationalism, yet there is no hard evidence that suggests that the members of the Nation of Islam carry any recognized political power either locally or nationally. Even the black congressional caucus seems to have little, if any, real political power.

Second, for all that has been said about black economic self-sufficiency, the reality is that black national-

---

[3] Joe R. Feagin Copyright 1994 by Grolier Electronic Publishing, Inc.

ism lacks economic clout. Consider the fact that, according to a recent report on wealth in America (NBC News, July 1995), the top half of all black people have assets of fifty-eight thousand dollars. The bottom half have less than four hundred dollars in assets. It is noteworthy that, for the most part, the black Muslim ideology is most effective among the inner city poor and college and university students. To the extent that the Nation of Islam embodies the idea of contemporary black nationalism, it can be argued that the higher one climbs up the social and economic ladder the less nationalistic blacks tend to be.

The African American parent must give attention to the current popularity of black nationalism on the college and university campuses in view of the fact that the evidence tends to suggest that in white America, black nationalism does not fit well with political power and economic clout. A friend of mine put it this way, "Nationalism is nothing less than a bad myth in a country driven by economics." While black nationalism has its value and should not be dismissed as insignificant, the dangers inherent in it also must not be overlooked.

Nationalism in any context is a reaction to oppression and persecution, both social and economic. This is most evident in the nation of Israel. There is hardly a nation that is more nationalistic than the nation of the Jews. This is no less true of black nationalism. It is a reaction to the oppression and persecution of black people in this country. Thus the African American parent whose goal it is to grow a proactive adult will struggle with the reactive spirit of nationalism.

In addition to promising more than it can deliver, black nationalism contains significant assumptions that lead to futility. *First it infers in its message the idea that black people are a monolithic group.* It is not uncommon to hear black nationalists speak as if the values, goals, and life-style they ascribe to are the same for all black people. The fact is, in many instances, the only thing some black people have in common is that they are members of the same race. There is nothing monolithic at all about black people, not even their genetic make up. The African-American parent must keep in focus the fact that their child is an individual that belongs to a family with a history that is unique. The values, lifestyle, and Christian convictions of the African American child are rooted in the distinctives of their family. African American children must be trained to see themselves as those who are a part of a diverse black community with a rich heritage.

The second futile assumption that black nationalism makes is that all blacks start from the same point in life economically, domestically, educationally, and socially. While it may make good copy to the news media to suggest that all black people started from the same point in life, it cannot be substantiated with fact. There is as much difference between the different social and economic class groups among black people as there is among white people in terms of social and economic mobility. The children of different class groups have different starting points in life. This means that black children differ significantly in the kind of help they need to succeed in life.

Third, black nationalism carries the futile assumption that all black people have the same goals in life. In truth, however, diversity is more the reality among black people. Thus the African American parent must strive to pass on to their children goals that fit with their child's individual ambition. This means being willing to be what one is in spite of what people think one ought to be because he or she is black. In spite of the personal values contained in black nationalism, and there are many, there are some real dangers to which African American parents must give serious attention.

The Christian family faces additional problems with black nationalism. First, it tends to be anti-Christian in that it exalts Islam with a sprinkling of Christian ideology. Nationalism becomes a part of the worldview of young black people to that extent that they question with a view to reject Christ as God, the Bible as the Word of God and Christianity as a religion of choice for black people in America. Among black students on the college campuses, the Koran is far more popular than the Bible. As a pastor, I cannot count the number of students who left for college with faith in Christ only to return with faith in the Koran, having had their Christian faith shipwrecked by Islamic teachings under the guise of nationalism.

Black nationalism is profitable in many ways at the personal level. However, it must always be kept in subjection to the mandate of Scripture which place oneness in

Christ above race. The Bible embraces the idea of nationalism. This can be seen in Deuteronomy 6 in God's instruction to the Jews as to how to parent their children so that they knew who He was and who they were. However in Christ, unity that transcends race is the priority.

ACCULTURATION

In his book *The Rage of a Privileged Class: Why Are Middle-Class Blacks Angry? Why Should America Care?* Cose wrote the following,

> While it's no doubt true that removing people from slums and placing them in a more wholesome environment could go a long way towards reducing crime (if only because it would expose some young delinquents to a more productive set of goals), it doesn't follow that it would do much to reduce alienation. Many well-educated, affluent blacks have already found their way out of inner-city ghettoes, yet they have note escaped America's myriad racial demons. Consequently, they remain either estranged or in a state of emotional turmoil.[4]

The African American parent must operate with the understanding that their children must be equipped to function in a social and economic context that will demand and accept their acculturation into whiteness but will at the same time deny assimilation into the white social and economic context.

Cose writes further, "For most blacks in America, regardless of status, political persuasion, or accomplishment, the moment never arrives when race can be treated as a total irrelevancy. Instead, too often it is the only relevant factor defining our existence."[5] It would be wonderful if I could respond to Cose and say such is not the case for Christian African American parents in their relationship with white believers. Unfortunately, however, I cannot disagree with him.

While there are a few blacks who are viewed by the white community as safe blacks and therefore are privy to social, cultural, and economic assimilation (at least in a

---

[4] Ellis Cose, *The Rage of a Privileged Class: Why Are Middle-Class Blacks Angry?* (Harper Collins, 1993), p. 28.

[5] Ibid.

limited sense), the fact is most African Americans will attest to the truth in Mr. Cose statement.

According to Cose, the following quote came from David Dinkins, former mayor of the city of New York. "A white man with a million dollars is a millionaire, and a black man with a million dollars is a nigger with a million dollars." He continues, "New York mayor David Dinkins told me over lunch in October 1992 attributing the aphorism to his friend Percy Sutton, the former Manhattan borough president. Dinkins quickly added that he wasn't sure Sutton was the source, and also made clear that the view expressed was not necessarily his own. Yet I suspect the statement captured a sentiment and a resentment, that burned brightly in Dinkin's heart." [6]

The African American parent will do well to train their children to deal with the rage that will likely show up in them by the time they reach the second year of college or by the time they reach their early twenties. This internal rage most often has the power to stifle or even destroy the motivation of the child to pursue certain careers.

This rage results from the fact that acculturation in America is deceptive, for it does not deliver on its assumed promise of assimilation. Dealing with this rage means being tough enough to strive against whatever the odds to attain your desired objective.

William lived in a predominantly white suburb of a major city and worked for a prestigious company. As an executive in the company, William developed friendships among his associates who were mostly white and both his children and their children grew up together. When William's son reached his teens, things begin to change for him in that his father's friends began to sense that he was increasingly interested in dating their daughters. The idea of a black boy dating their white daughters was, for William's friends, not a part of the acculturation they had demanded and accepted from him.

The limitation of acculturation of blacks to white culture has serious limitations for both parent and children. The African American parent must raise their children with these limitations in view.

---

[6] Ibid.

Part 3

Roles and Relationships in Parenting African American Children

CHAPTER 10

THE ROLE OF THE AFRICAN AMERICAN FATHER

When Daniel Patrick Moynihan wrote his report on the black family thirty years ago he described it as "a tangle of pathology." Listed among the cause of the pathology, or deviation from the norm, of the black family was what Moynihan referred to as its "matriarchal structure." This structure was said to be contrary to the basic American family structure. Thus, according to Moynihan, the future of the black family had nothing but pathology as its destiny.[1]

Historically speaking, what Moynihan said was not true of the black family. Black women did not function as the authority figure in the home. The father did. While it has most often been the case that white men tended to disregard the black man in deference to the black woman, the black woman always knew who was the authority in the home. She has always chosen to respect her husband because of who he was as an individual and in spite of how he was treated by white people. Matriarchy was historically not a reality in the black family.

Today in terms of economics, the black man ranks low in annual income, behind the white man, the black

---

[1] *The Moynihan Report: The Politics of Controversy*, MIT, 1967.

-85-

woman, and white woman. This economic reality gives the impression that the black woman is the primary authority in the home because, in many instances, she is the primary bread winner. However, as it has always been historically, the black woman must, in the tradition of her mother, choose to respect her husband in spite of his economic rank in the home.

The real issue today is not male authority in the home but male presence in the home. The fact is more than half of all black children today are born into homes where there is no resident father. When this happens the only authority in the home is the mother. While mothers may on occasion grow strong and successful sons and daughters, they are not as well-equipped to parent without the father.

In terms of parenting, Jocelyn Elders, former Surgeon General of the United States, said it best when she said that fathers must contribute more than sperm to the parenting process. I am in full agreement with this statement.

First, the father must take primary responsibility in nurturing the spiritual life of the child. In the black church black women outnumber black men eight to one. This means that for every eight black women who attend church there is only one black man. By contrast, in the Nation of Islam, black men outnumber the women at about the same percentage. It is a small wonder that the Islamic faith is increasingly the religion of choice of young black men. The fact is, sons tend to imitate their fathers.

Fathers need to pay more attention to nurturing the spiritual lives of their sons. When young men reach their teens they often stop going to church, choosing in many instances to become a Muslim. The alternative to this spiritual failure is that fathers take the primary responsibility for the spiritual development of their children.

Colossians 3:21 says, "Fathers, do not exasperate your children, that they may not lose heart." To avoid provoking anger in their children fathers must avoid attitudes, words, and actions which drive a child to anger and cause resentment to build. Fathers must avoid excessive discipline, unreasonably harsh demands, abusing their authority, arbitrariness, unfairness, and constant nagging and condemnation, thus subjecting the child to humiliation. Fathers must not be insensitive to the needs and feelings of the child.

Someone has well said that a child should not be corrected by hurting but by persuading. For some reason it seems that the African American father believes that the only way to correct their sons is by hurting them emotionally, physically, or even economically. The idea seems to be that the correcting is in the hurting.

In an article published in the Dallas Morning News on March 17, 1995 entitled "Black Boys Need High Expectations," by Leonard Pitts, the following story is told.

Mike was a "nigger" and because of that he never would amount to much. He knew that because his father told him so. Greg was a white boy, and though he faced daunting obstacles, he could realize his dreams if he just worked hard. He too was told that by his father. Mike drifted through the company of pimps, whores, thieves, and drug dealers and was blinded in a barroom shooting in 1974. Greg became a teacher and a lawyer, earned a Ph.D. and now is dean of a law school.

What may surprise you is that they are brothers of the same parents. Their mother was white. Their father, of mixed racial descent was also mixed-up emotionally, torn by the destructive passions of a light-skinned black man passing for white. Perhaps it was this self-loathing that caused him to encourage one son and revile another, though both of his sons looked as "black" as a white person. The African American father may have learned a method of parenting his sons that is inherently destructive to that son. It turns him into an angry child who grows into an angry man.

In Colossians 3:21b the text says, "that they may not lose heart." What does it means to lose heart? A child who has lost heart is a child who has been broken in spirit. When a child goes through the day in a listless, moody, and sullen frame of mind, then that child is demonstrating the characteristics of brokenness of spirit.

Brokenness has three basic characteristics. First, it evidences a sense of hopelessness crouched in a spirit of inward rage; second, a loss of self-esteem crouched in an attitude of insecurity; and third, a persistent state of depression combined with a fear of being alone.

It is totally within the reach of any father to so exasperate their children, especially their sons, so that they lose heart and become as a walking time bomb.

There is an alternative to growing angry sons (note the text) "but bring them up in the nurture and instruction of the Lord." This word "nourish" is used in Ephesians 5:29 with reference to how a man treats his own body. In that context we understand that to nourish the body one must include such things as a proper diet, medical care, spiritual development, physical exercise, and sufficient sleep. In other words, a man knows and does what is necessary to take good care of himself.

Black men are not nourishing their bodies very well. They are dying from cancer more than ever before, specifically lung cancer. Lung cancer is one of the most preventable cancers around yet our men are dying from it. The prevention is do not smoke. Black men today—to a greater extent than ever before—are alcoholics. One of the reasons they are not helped is because they refuse to get help. They feel they do not need any help. Black men are killing themselves at an alarming rate today. Suicide among black men is a growing problem.

To the extent that to nurture means to care for oneself well and holistically, black men are obviously not doing well. Now since it can be said that what a man does for himself, he will do no more than that for others. It can then be concluded that when it comes to nurturing his children black men have a real problem. The problem is bringing the child up in the nurture and admonition of the Lord when he does less than that for himself.

The second primary responsibility of the father is to transmit the family values to the children. Family values include such things as ethics, morality, work ethic, and respect for others. While these principles are certainly not taught by the father without the support and involvement of the mother, it is his primary responsibility.

A few facts must not be overlooked as we consider the role of the father in parenting today. First, black youth have a 50 percent higher probability of dying before age twenty than youth of other races in this country. Second, the most frequent cause of death among black youths include homicide, drug abuse, suicide, and accidents. Third, 30 percent of all black youth in American drop out of school before the ninth grade. Fourth, 42 percent of all homicide victims in America are black and most of the murders of blacks are committed by blacks. Finally, only

33 percent of black youths go on to college after graduating from high school. These are sobering realities.

In terms of parenting, we may be doing quite well as individual parents in our own little houses but as a race of people and as a community we are not doing well at all. The missing ingredient is all too often a father who both knows his role and fills it.

Much is said today about the environment in which children grow up. The idea seems to be that the general negative social, economic, and moral environment in which today's children are raised is the primary cause of their high level of failure. To be sure, a negative environment will impact children in many ways. However, nurture is far more significant in terms of the values children will hold as adults than is the environment in which they grew up.

In the August 1994 issue of *Time* magazine, my hometown was listed as the poorest city in America. It is hardly possible for anyone to have grown up in a social and political environment that was more negative than the one in which I grew up. Yet the things I value most as an adult African American male include family, education, a strong work ethic, a middle class lifestyle, and my Christian faith. These and many other things I hold dear are a result of the nurturing I received from my parents, in spite of the negative environment in which I grew up. My father was a man of principles and he passed on to me the ideas he treasured most. As an example, my father would not wear any clothing that was not made by top-of-the-line manufacturers. All of his clothes had to have a certain label in them indicating to him that they were of the highest quality or he simply would not wear them. Most of my Dad's clothes were tailor-made. This value on quality clothes is woven into the very fabric of my value system. I find myself avoiding clothes that do not have certain labels in them.

The third primary responsibility of the father is to provide for the economic needs of his children. In July 1989, a select committee on children, youth and families from the U.S. House of Representatives held a hearing on "Barriers and Opportunities for America's Young Black Men." Of the many conclusions reached about black children, two are worth noting here. First, in terms of the financial support African American men provide for their children, there is a direct relationship between the employment of African American men and the amount of money provided to their children. Men who have jobs that provide adequate income tended to support their families. Second, it was determined that there is a direct relationship between black female-headed households and unemployment of black men.

The notion that African American men are simply irresponsible as fathers, contributing nothing more than sperm to the parenting process lacks substance when viewed through the lens of the economic status of black men in this country.

Having been in ministry for more than thirty years and also being a father of three children, it is clear to me that there is a direct relationship between a man's ability to exercise authority in his home and his ability to provide for that home. In this area the African American father has a problem. On average he earns less than his wife does. Yet he is responsible before God to be the primary bread winner for his family.

In an article published some time ago entitled "Black Men: An Endangered Species, Who's Really Pulling the Trigger?" the author said, "Black parents should spend more time raising their male children. In many families sons do not receive the nurturing that their daughters receive. Boys are allowed too much freedom to decide their life-style, educational goals, and careers. As a consequence, many black men never reach their full potential. Black parents, especially fathers, must invest more quality time and energy in raising sons."[2] While it may not be possible to flip the economic scales overnight so that black men are equal to white men in annual income, it is possible for the parents of black boys to do a better job in pushing them to develop to their full potential.

Fourth, the African American father must provide for and contribute to the education of the child. My father was functionally illiterate and yet he had a passion for education and he passed that passion on to his children. A

---

[2] Thomas Parham and Roderick J. McDavis, "Black Men, An Endangered Species: Who's Really Pulling the Trigger?" *Journal of Counseling and Development* 66 (September 1987), pp. 24-27.

number of African American fathers will do everything possible to educate their daughters but will contribute very little to the education of their sons, even in public school. The general idea seems to be that boys must be able to make it on their own. For many black boys this means getting a job at an age in which they are very susceptible to the ways of the world.

The father must involve himself in the overall educational environment of the child. This means from kindergarten through college the father is just as involved in the decisions, events, achievements, and struggles of the child as is the mother. One could argue that boys demand more involvement from the father in the public school environment in view of the large number of women teachers in the classroom through elementary school.

It is the opinion of some that in the black community the primary disciplinarian in the home is the mother. I disagree with this opinion in general. However I am of the opinion that, while in single families the mother is an effective disciplinarian with daughters, this does not seem to be the case with sons. In the home the primary disciplinarian needs to be the father. In doing so, the father teaches the child respect for authority as well as respect for manhood.

The father is best equipped to develop in the child survival skills for life. Wisdom is best taught by the father to the children and from heart to heart, not head to head. The wisdom of which I speak is the ability to distinguish between that which seems to be important but is not and that which seems to be important and really is. The father who fathers well teaches the child how to survive in a social system. This means participating in the development of the child's social skills both as a model and also as one who bends the will of the child to accommodate the family value system. In addition the father who fathers well teaches the child how to think critically. Critical thinking is the ability to look back at yesterday and make some sense of today and to look at today and gain insight into tomorrow. Critical thinking means seeing more than what is evident, hearing more than what is said, and feeling more than what is bothering you.

The final primary responsibility of the father is to demonstrate love and commitment to the mother of the child. I discovered quite by accident that my children did not gain a sense of security in my love for them by what I said to them nor did they gain such confidence by what I did for them. My children gained their unwavering confidence in my love for them by observing how much I love their mother. The father who fathers must learn to love his children through their mother.

I find it more than a little bit interesting that most of the men I have counseled over the past thirty years who physically and emotionally abused their wives were men whose father physically and emotionally abused their mother. The most insecure women I have counseled over the years are women who had no model of a father loving their mother. I therefore conclude that there is a connection between the perceived love of a father for his child and the relationship between the father and the mother of that child.

It has long been established that the converse of the female-headed household in the African American community is the number of unemployed and underemployed black men. In addition, the converses of the raging violent black on black crime involving youths is the absence of an effective father. Black men must come to grips with the fact that fathering demands more of him than his sperm.

CHAPTER 11

THE ROLE OF THE AFRICAN AMERICAN MOTHER

As it pertains to the absence of African American fathers, we have a serious crisis on our hands. The absentee father is a major social problem in our day that seems to have no immediate solution. We must keep working to correct this problem. However as it relates to motherhood, Exodus chapter two provides us with a few excellent insights into the impact of motherhood. In this passage it is important to observe that in regards to what God was doing in terms of preserving and shaping the life of Moses, all of the primary players were women.

The women first included the midwives who chose to disobey the edict of the Pharaoh which was to kill at birth all male babies born to Jewish women. Second, there was Moses' mother Jochebed who hid him for three months in the house. Third, there was Moses' sister Miriam who, when asked to find a Jewish woman to nurse the infant baby Moses, went and got Moses' mother to do that job. Finally, there was the daughter of the Pharaoh who adopted Moses as her own son and raised him in the Egyptian palace. As we look at Moses' early life, all of the primary players are women.

Moses was conceived and born into a social environment in which the edict of death hung over the Jewish community like a dark cloud on a stormy day. In the book of Acts chapter seven, Stephen testifies to the fact that after Joseph died in Egypt, the Jews lost their favor with the Egyptian Pharaoh and steps were taken to take advantage of the Jewish race by the new Pharaoh. One of the cruel measures taken against the Jewish people was what Stephen in Acts 7 referred to as the exposure of the infant Jewish boys so that they died. It was in this violent social context that Moses was born. The Pharaoh knew well that the key to killing off the Jewish race was eliminating all the sons of Jewish mothers.

God created Moses in the womb of his mother during the time that the government had legalized the killing of all Jewish infant boys. The issue however was not what the government had mandated but rather how much of a priority did Moses' mother put on mothering.

The whole of African American family history from the slave ships to the plantations, to Jim Crow right through to today, testifies to the fact that motherhood does not rest in the hands of circumstances nor is it necessarily threatened by social, economic, or political crisis. Motherhood, historically for the African American mother, stands or falls on the commitment of the mother to mothering.

Moses' birth occurred at a time when the nation of Israel was caught in its most serious struggle for survival. Genocide was in the air and, if left unchallenged, it would in time wipe out the whole Jewish nation. It was here that Moses mother, along with the midwives, decided that, in spite of the edict of the Pharaoh, they would cast their vote in favor of motherhood. These women decided to challenge the system.

Today the African American community is caught in a similar situation. In an unofficial edict, the government seems to have declared that black boys will be destroyed somewhere in their early childhood. In this context of violence against black children, some mothers seem to have gone into coalition with the government. The abortionist's tools are all too commonly a part of the cycle of violence perpetuated upon black children. The language of a growing number of women today contains the statement "unwanted pregnancy." This means that it is better to have an abortion than to bring an unwanted child into the world and abuse or neglect it. Yes, there were black women who opted to abort their infants rather than have them born into slavery. However, this was not the solution to the slave problem. It was those women who mothered their children in spite of the environment that produced the men and women who saved the black race from annihilation and brought an end to slavery.

Jochebed teaches us that children are part and parcel of who and what a mother is. More importantly, she teaches us that when a race of people find themselves in a serious crisis, whether social, political, or otherwise, the people of God should expect God to raise up a deliverer and every mother should treat motherhood as if she could be the mother of that deliverer. In other words, every mother should see her role as a partner with the living God in growing children. This means mothering from the point of view that when there is a crisis in the land the Christian mother, no matter her socio-economic status, treats her pregnancy as if the child she is carrying is the leader that God will use to deliver His people.

Through divine providence Moses' mother was given the privilege to nurse her son for three years, after which she gave him back to the daughter of Pharaoh. For the next thirty-seven years of his life, Moses was educated, treated, and lived as an Egyptian. Moses looked, dressed, thought, and lived like an Egyptian for thirty-seven years of his life. However, when Moses reached age forty, something happened inside his heart and he felt compelled to visit the community of his people. What Moses mother did in the first three years of his life could not be erased by thirty-seven years of living as an Egyptian. In other words, it was the effective mothering of Moses' mother that stood guard over his heart in spite of the way in which he had been trained to live. You see, on the outside Moses was made an Egyptian by his adopted Egyptian mother but on the inside his mother had made him a Jew. It was not possible for Moses to separate himself from the effective mothering of his poor and oppressed mother.

There are several specific responsibilities mothers should prioritize in parenting. *First, mothers should manage the home environment and the general early education of the children.* This means maintaining a home environment in which hearts are more important than heads, and feelings are more evident that are agenda's. Mothers should teach their children the basic relational skills, sensitivities, and the fundamentals of education. This responsibility is best fitted for the first three years of the child's life.

Second, mothers are to teach by example compassion, tenderness, and love. There is little disagreement over the general fact that black mothers love their children. However, it is increasingly evident that black mothers are not growing children who are capable of loving. What may be missing in today's mothering is the model of a loving compassionate, tender-hearted mother. It seems to me that motherhood must include an example of the softer side of life. This is not to suggest that fathers need not be loving and compassionate because they must be. However, women seem to be designed by God to be tenderhearted and compassionate and to be the best examples of such.

Third, mothers should set specific goals for their children. The mother is many times the first of the parents to recognize the talents and potential of the child. It may well be that mothers also have some divine illumination as to the purpose for which that child was born. Thus it seems to me that mothers are well-fitted to tailoring the agenda, exposure and boundaries of the child according to the child's emerging personality. The history and present day testimonies of African Americans are replete with stories of mothers who set specific goals for their children and developed them accordingly.

Motherhood means nurturing the spirit of the child. There is the serious need of every child to have a mother who is able to restore and reinforce the spirit of the children when they succeed or fail. The mother is often the buffer between the harsh world in which the child lives and the inner spirit. The child who has no mother to nurture its spirit will most often develop into an adult that is low in self-esteem.

Finally the mother must train the child in interpersonal skill and social norms. Learning how to get along with others is an essential part of growing up balanced. This means learning to communicate, listen, and respond in a positive manner. It means learning to settle disagreements without hurting the person with whom you disagree.

CHAPTER 12

THE ROLE OF THE AFRICAN AMERICAN CHURCH

There are few institutions in the African American community that have played as significant a role in the lives of black people as the black church has. It is interesting to note that in the stereotypes of the black family and community, the black woman is perceived as the dominant force and yet the one institution that embodies the hope, strength, and survival of black people is led by black men. Most pastors in the black community are black men.

Women make up the largest proportion of the active membership of black churches and yet the church constitution by-laws and internal relationships are ordered by men. Men are the chief power-holders in the church and the denominational hierarchies, although increasingly, black women are leading churches. For the most part though, the black church is a male-dominated institution that is heavily populated by women.

Today more than ever before there is a growing indifference and intolerance on the part of black men toward the black church. Yet the history of the black church attests to the fact that black men have benefited in the most positive ways from the ministry of the black church.

Historically, black men who had experienced the negative lifestyle of hopelessness and oppression have found spiritual and psychological liberation in the church. During the days of slavery and Jim Crow laws, it was the black church that recognized black men as men and helped to develop their leadership abilities. The black church developed black men intellectually so that they were able to contribute to the good of society. The concept of family had been virtually stripped away from the moral code of black men through studding and other breeding practices. The black church restored the idea of family to the masses of black men. Black men have also been excluded from the main line of economic achievement. Through the black church, they have developed economic enterprises and learned to compete and succeed. Finally, the black church taught them how to network among themselves as well as among other races. These men owe a great deal to the church. It has always been a significant part of the black family and the black community.

However, while the black church has contributed significantly to the survival and development of black men, it is suffering today from what it has not done. First, the black church has not provided a meaningful role for laymen and non-pastors. There are few black churches that have the internal mechanism with which nonministerial members can be given a voice in the church that is equal to the pastor's voice. Second, the black church tends to espouse a kind of psychological passivity that is inconsistent with the basic nature of black men. Third, the black church tends to advocate a prohibitive gospel message as opposed to a liberating gospel. Finally, the black church has not developed a comprehensive ministry to college and university students, nor has it developed a significant ministry to prisons or the armed services.

There are specific responsibilities that the black church has to the black family that must be mentioned. The role of the church in the parenting of African American children is to guide the family in bringing together the spiritual, social, domestic, economic, and political dimensions of life. In its ministry of guiding in parenting, the church must first assume the responsibility of reinforcing the spiritual values and lifestyle taught at home. This reinforcing is best done through the model of a Christian home that the church produces through its ministry. At the top of the list of models of Christian values and lifestyle are the pastor, officers, and other church leaders.

It must be recognized that there is a shortage of the type of family structures defined as the nuclear family in which there are two parents with their children. This type of family structure is not restricted to the Christian community since it must be acknowledged that, from a biblical perspective, this is the ideal divinely-ordained family structure. Thus contributing to the development of nuclear family models must be a primary goal of the church.

Second, the church must through its discipleship and Christian education programs develop the spiritual foundation laid by the father in the home. This includes salvation, morality, forgiveness, compassion, and love. The church must take the responsibility of developing its ministry to the families to the point that it offers more than a weekly worship experience. The staff must be equipped to indoctrinate the family. Failure to develop the spiritual foundation of the children is the primary cause behind the success of the non-Christian Islamic faith among black youth on college and university campuses.

Third, the church must provide a meaningful worship experience for the whole family. Church worship services must be relevant for the contemporary context of today's family. Meaningful worship experiences means providing the atmosphere and content in which the heart, mind, and spirit are lifted in praise to the living God.

Fourth, the church must provide Christian education for the family. In the black church, Christian education has primarily been limited to Sunday school. which unfortunately, is in more than a few instances an exercise in biblical ignorance by a few diligent good people that love the Lord but who are ill-equipped to teach. Christian education is the serious business of equipping saints of all ages to walk with God in the context in which they live.

Fifth, the church must have an effective ministry of shepherding the whole family. The social and economic context in which black people must parent is such that they need shepherding. This includes counseling, modeling, encouraging, and even rebuking when necessary.

While many who are writing about the black family no longer see a role for the church, especially in parenting, the church is still the most important institution in the black community and is uniquely fitted for the task of equipping black parents to parent.

CHAPTER 13

THE ROLE OF AFRICAN AMERICAN CHILDREN

Every child needs both the time and environment conducive to being a child. It takes time to grow into adulthood. Thus the role of the child is to be a child.

For some time now, a growing number of black children in every social class appear to be skipping their childhood. Boys and girls are moved by circumstances, attitude, parents, and other sources of influence from infancy to adulthood. Teenage girls today dress, date, talk, entertain, and have babies as adult women do. So do teenage boys. However, due to the fact that boys on the average develop physically slower than girls, it is more difficult for young boys to look like men than it is for young girls to look like women. It has become difficult to recognize and distinguish between the children and the parents because they all tend to dress, think, and act alike. This is a serious problem in parenting that must be changed. Children can only be what they are, namely children. Parents who disregard this fact fragment the soon-to-be adult.

Maggie was a fragmented adult. She could never seem to act the part of a responsible adult. She tended to always need someone to act as her parent and give her unlimited attention. Maggie's dependent attitude frustrated her husband Bill. Maggie's problem was that she never had the opportunity to be a child. Her home environment as a child forced her to grow up too fast and pushed her into adult parenting responsibilities before her tenth birthday. By the time Maggie reached her teens, she was carrying the parenting responsibilities of an adult woman. As a child, Maggie had the full responsibility of caring for several children, even though she had no children of her own.

There is a national crisis that has emerged referred to as "children at risk." The focus of this crisis is children who are having children. The evidence suggests that a growing number of teenage girls are intentionally getting pregnant. These teen mothers say that the reason for the pregnancy is so they can have someone to love them unconditionally and that they can love. In reality it seems as if these children have determined that it is better to have a real baby than a doll to mother. They seem oblivious to the fact that having a baby, unlike a doll, ends their childhood and plunges them into the arena of full-blown motherhood with all the responsibilities that go with it.

When one considers the ineptness of teen mothers in their mothering it is evident that children are ill-equipped to parent. These children need to be parented themselves. Social workers and law enforcement officers around the country tend to agree that the children of teen mothers are often neglected, abused, and develop into violent youths and adults. This result further confirms that children are only equipped to be children even though they may look and act like adults.

The Bible teaches in Psalm 90 that a normal life span for the average person is seventy years. Taking these seventy years and dividing them into four quarters of twenty years plus in each, it could be said that the first twenty years of a person's life should be spent growing up. In this first twenty years an individual is to learn how to live the remaining fifty years. Should it be that this twenty year training program is disrupted, aborted, or otherwise negatively impacted, the resultant adult will likely be fragmented and ill-equipped to parent as an adult.

Children need time to mature in mind, body, and spirit. Thus parents must strive to provide an atmosphere in which their children can mature holistically. Children should have the liberty to dream, fantasize, and think wild and crazy thoughts. Children should have a place to go where they can simply be alone to think. They should not have to worry about how they are going to survive in

Parenting in the Context of a Spiritual Deficit

terms of food, clothing, and housing. Parents owe them all of that. Parents owe their children unconditional love fitted to each child's individual personality. It is not their responsibility to provide for their education. Security and provision are the responsibility of the parents.

Otis was a man who would tell you that he has worked all of his life. According to Otis, he began working as a young boy mowing lawns to earn money to buy his school clothes. Thus as a parent, Otis believed that his children must earn their living by working. Otis was not aware that most of the excessive material possessions he purchased and kept at his house reflected the desires of his missed childhood. As an adult man, Otis often made decisions and acted like an irresponsible boy. The point is, it is important that children have a childhood.

The responsibility of the child is threefold. *First, the child is responsible for placing high value on their parents as parents.* In all too many instances the parent places more value on the child as their child than the child places on the parent as their parent. Some children seem to believe that it is their parent's privilege to have them as their child. Thus the child proceeds to order the parent around as if he or she were the adult. There have even been cases where children literally hit their parents when they did not get what they wanted.

The role of the child must be clearly distinguished from the role of the parent in the mind of both the parent and the child. This means as a parent loving the child so much that you bend its will so that the child is both respectful and obedient. This means teaching the child respect for authority and respect for the rights of others.

Clearly in the Scriptures the attitude of the child is to be one of respect for his or her parents. Out of this respect comes a spirit of obedience to the parents. I cannot accept the idea that a child who has been carried in its mother's womb for nine months and having been totally dependent upon his parents for all of its needs has the liberty to disrespect his or her parents. The Bible commands children to respect their parents.

Jamie was the child of her mother's extramarital affair. Her father had nothing to do with her childhood. In elementary school Jamie began to succeed in athletics. By the time she reached high school she was a recognized track and field competitor. It was at this point that her father begin to claim her as his daughter. However, by this time Jamie had grown to hate her father and resented everything she knew about him. When I met Jamie her father was on his death bed, dying of cancer. He had been calling for her everyday as he grew weaker and drew closer to death. Yet Jamie had refused to see her father.

In my conversation with Jamie, she asked my opinion of what she should do in view of the fact that her father was dying. As I listened to Jamie's story of resentment and hatred combined with a longing to have a father in her life, I was reminded again of how important it is for children to be able to value their parents.

Second, the child has a responsibility to learn and grow and parents are responsible for the welfare of their children. This means that children should not be compelled to take a job to earn their own living. The problem with children in the workplace is that minimum wage jobs often at fast food places, tend to stifle the intellectual, emotional, and spiritual development of the child.

Over the years black boys who get low paying jobs with the idea of working a few hours inevitably wind up working long hours to make more money. The long hours are just one of the problems with black boys in the marketplace. The major problem is the first thing many boys do with their few dollars is buy a cheap car that they cannot afford to take care of so they wind up getting a second job to make more money. The result of all of this can be that the teenage boy winds up losing his childhood, stifling his intellectual development, and often flunking out of school. Parents should place more value on the overall growth and development of their children than they do on their children getting a job.

The scenario is slightly different with teenage girls who are pushed prematurely into the workforce. Most often they continue to grow but all too often become the prey of older men who ruin their future by getting them into exploitative moral situations. Children are to be held to the responsibility of growing up and not much else.

I am not suggesting that children should not work at all, but rather that work should be a secondary consideration. Priority should be given to the overall growth and development of a child.

Parenting In The Context Of A Spiritual Deficit

Finally, children are responsible for nurturing within their own hearts a spirit of hope with anticipation of a positive tomorrow. A number of children reach their teen years without any hope of a future. Children tend to think only of today and their immediate wants. Life is so difficult for some children that it robs them of hope before reaching the age of sixteen.

Parents should strive with all of their might to give their children the kind of positive and secure environment in the home that will keep hope alive in the child no matter the environment in which they live. To this end parents must be positive about life in general and must be stable in their relationship with each other.

The child who has no hope of a tomorrow in which they are an active, positive participant will, in all likelihood, not prepare for it. Thus parents must give the child the opportunity to develop hope in a positive environment.

Preaching To The Wind: No Excuse For Flunking Life

I grew up in the South in the midst of the horrors of segregation and white supremacy. Life was hard and dangerous. My parents were good people who went to church but were also given to open physical fighting. My sisters and brothers and I often fought among ourselves as well as with other children in the neighborhood. Yet we all grew up with a sense of pride and purpose. We loved life and were most often full of hope. Sometimes I think that I have more hope than all the others because, unlike my older brother, I as the youngest had the privilege of being a child. So I dreamed and I valued my parents. I grew up and I have never stop learning even as an adult.

One of the realities that must be faced as Christians, no matter a person's age and regardless of whether they are a child or a parent, is that oppression in the form of racism and discrimination still exists in our society. The fact that it is not popular to talk about it does not change the fact of its existence. One of the strongest evidences of the reality of racial oppression in this country is that unemployment is highest among black men and black youth throughout this country. In reality, corporate America evidences a propensity for giving most to its jobs to men and youth of other races, choosing to leave the black community both under- and unemployed.

Given this set of circumstances caused primarily by racism, many of our youth concede to failure and ultimately learn to like it. These young people come to the conclusion that, given their circumstances, it is all right to give up on life and just do nothing. However, being a young oppressed minority is no excuse for flunking life.

By flunking life, I mean arriving at adulthood without having successfully acquired the necessary emotional, spiritual, and intellectual skills to successfully play the game of life and win no matter the oppressive context in which you must live. You must not survey the current social and economic oppressive situation in America and decide not to try. As a young African American, you must decide that no matter the oppressive nature of the context, quitting for you is not an option.

The first step in flunking life is the failure to develop personal spiritual convictions that will sustain and protect you morally, ethically, and with integrity. In any context these virtues are invaluable, but even in an oppressive society.

The second step in flunking life is failure to become literate and productive. It must be understood that life in an oppressive context will not forgive one's functional illiteracy. One cannot participate in the marketplace with such limitations. For the illiterate, an oppressive society builds prisons and homeless shelters as means of retaining and maintaining them as underclass people.

The third step in flunking life involves growing up an emotional cripple, unable to deal with oppressive situations such as opposition, discrimination, and rejection in a constructive way. In an oppressive society it is necessary to be thick-skinned and long on persistence. It is therefore necessary to know what you want to do with your life.

To avoid flunking life in an oppressive society young black boys must determine before God and make a firm commitment before God not to wind up in prison, hooked on drugs, or being an unwed father. By the same token black girls must vow before God and commit themselves to a moral standard that will prevent them from getting pregnant. They must commit themselves to abstaining from sex until marriage.

PARENTING IN THE CONTEXT OF A SPIRITUAL DEFICIT

In 521 B.C., Jerusalem and the entire Southern Kingdom of Israel was captured by the Babylonians. Subsequent to their capture the Jewish people became an oppressed minority among the Babylonian people. The reigning king of the time was Nebuchadnezzar who was himself revered as a god by the Babylonian people.

In capturing the Jewish people, King Nebuchadnezzar decided to take a few of the Jewish boys and make them productive leaders in the Babylonian kingdom. To accomplish this goal the king ordered that these boys be given new names and a Babylonian education which included language, arts. and religion.

One of the Jewish boys who was taken was named Daniel. Though the Bible does not specify Daniel's age at the time he and the other boys were taken, it is most likely that he was a teenage boy. Daniel was taken from his parents, friends, and culture and carried off to Babylon to become a servant in the kingdom of the Babylonian people.

In Babylon Daniel was not just a minority, he was an oppressed minority in that he had no rights, no family and no apparent future as a Jewish man among his own people. In this context Daniel was most likely castrated, perhaps to prevent his intermarrying with the Babylonian people. Yet for Daniel the fact that he was a young oppressed minority was no excuse for flunking life. Thus Daniel decided to succeed in life in spite of his oppressive circumstances.

Like most people who live in an oppressive situation Daniel had something going for him that his oppressive situation did not alter. The talents that Daniel brought to the kingdom of Babylon were talents that the Babylonians needed in order to survive and prosper as a great nation.

Daniel's abilities included a strong healthy body, that was well built and handsome. In Daniel's day as in our day a strong healthy good-looking person will get attention. In addition to his looks Daniel demonstrated the ability to apply himself to the study of wisdom. Daniel had abilities to learn in the areas of literature, language, and communication. Daniel's abilities included the physical, the mental, and the spiritual. These abilities were all necessary for Daniel to function effectively in the context in which he had been placed, which was the highest position in the service for the king.

Young people today must understand that talent and intellectual potential can be developed in spite of the social environment. However, there are few things that are as much of a threat to the development of talent and intellect than racism and discrimination.

These things include, but are not limited to, such things as becoming sexually active outside of marriage and thereby risking everything including life itself. A second danger is riotous living. Every teenage black female must keep in mind that the largest number of poor blacks in this country are single mothers. Children out of wedlock and loose living have the ever-present potential to wipe out every opportunity their talents can create for them. Thus, young black women must know that when they decide to let someone take advantage of them, they are putting their whole future on the line no matter how gifted they are.

Black boys must not be caught in the cycle of sport worship, automobile preoccupation, lusting for designer wear, and engaging in premarital sex that will make them fathers before they are ready to be a parent and a husband. These activities also go a long way towards destroying the development of intellect, emotions, and talents.

When the talents that the young man chooses to perfect, such as prowling the streets at night, are not in the arena of marketable skills, the young man flunks life and he flunks because of his own misplaced values.

Black youth must understand that of the great number of African American young men across this country who are excellent in various sports, less than one percent will ever get paid to play. Of those who get paid to play, only a very few of those will get paid well. Of those who are paid well, it is only for a very short period of time.

Of course, race-based social and economic oppression in this county are difficult adversaries but personal habits are far more devastating to the future of black youth in terms of their potential for success in an oppressive society. In this kind of society the oppressor tends not to forgive the oppressed minority youth for their failures as it does for the majority youth. The fact is, an undisciplined lifestyle and bad social habits combined with an unChristian attitude proves to be the far greater oppressor than are most racist systems.

PARENTING IN THE CONTEXT OF A SPIRITUAL DEFICIT

Many black youth have had the good fortune to grow up in church-oriented home environments. In addition as a people blacks have had the privilege of a rich religious heritage that sustained their forefathers through the cruelest form of oppression—slavery. Yet in terms of making it in life, it seems that many children have not benefited much from these privileges. Two essential things seem to be missing in the lives of these children—*spiritual convictions that are God-focused and faith in the living God through Jesus Christ.*

In the case of young Daniel, it is evident that he had a relationship with the living God and was given to studying the word of God. Daniel knew God and was committed to serving him in what ever environment he was in.

When it happened that he was snatched from his home and culture and was trained to serve in the highest and most prestigious position in Babylon, he took with him into this three-year university training all that he was in body, mind and spirit. Daniel somehow had the advantage of knowing that in an oppressive system as a minority, good looks, strong intellect, and significant talents were not sufficient. So Daniel took with him into that pagan, oppressive system his own strong, personal God-focused convictions wrapped in faith in the living God.

As a minority in an oppressed context Daniel, based on his own God focused convictions, made up his mind that he would not defile himself with the king's choice food and wine. Daniel recognized that he was a minority in an oppressive situation surrounded by heathens whose only interest in him was what good he could contribute to their survival and success.

In the religious setting in which Daniel had to live, to participate in the meal from the kings table meant to participate in the worship of the gods of Babylon. For Daniel this was not something he had the liberty to do.

It is an unfortunate reality that far too many young people reach their teen years already tainted with conformity to the world. What is worse, they have learned to worship at the shrine of physical sensuality where beauty is the sacrament of praise.

Far too many young people, while active church members, have not yet decided what they truly believe about God. Therefore these young people are without personal,

God-focused, spiritual convictions. This vacuum leaves them at the mercy of the pressure from their peers. Many of the peers of our children are beautiful and smart but in their hearts they are pagans, worshipping at the altar of immediate self-gratification.

It takes more than money, power, and good looks to make a man. Real men have convictions. Real life can be found only in Jesus Christ who said, "I have come that you might have life and have it more abundantly" (Jn. 10:10b).

No young African American male or female has the option to say they flunked life because of their race and their oppressive social, economic, and political environment. African American youth must bloom where they are.

Leonard was on his way to work one day when his car stalled about halfway between his job and his house. Leonard decided to walk back home and get help for his broken-down car. On his way home he decided to take a few short cuts through the back alleys that led to his house.

As he traveled through the alleys Leonard was struck by the awful smells and the accumulated trash that were in the alleys he was passing through. As he pondered the smells, and trash strewn throughout the alleys, Leonard's eyes suddenly fell upon a beautiful blooming tulip out there in that lonely, filthy alley.

Leonard stopped to observe the beauty of the tulip and while he was observing the tulip Leonard asked the tulip, "What is a beautiful tulip like yourself doing in an alley like this?" The tulip said, "I did not really know that this was an alley and it has always been as you see it now." "Well," said Leonard, "why are you blooming in this alley?" The tulip replied, "As I said, I really did not know I was in an alley, the only thing I know is that one day I discovered that I existed where I am and since this is where I was and relocating was not an option for me I decided to bloom where I am." African American youths must decide to bloom where they are no matter where that is.

CHAPTER 14

THE ROLE OF PARENTING IN FORMAL EDUCATION

The education of African American children is and will continue to be an issue of serious concern for many years to come. The focus of the discussion will undoubtedly shift but the issue will continue to be important.

Some conclude that there is a genetically-based cause behind the low performance of black children. Such conclusions are obviously biased and intend to keep alive the notion of the innate inferiority of black children and the superiority of white children.

This section is not about the various studies and results, as important as such studies are. It is about the role of parenting in the educational process. As an African American parent I have never had the privilege of assuming that education would just happen in the life of my child. Parents must realize that there is a strong possibility that their child also may be functionally illiterate should they simply leave the process to the educational institutions. There is a role that they have to fulfill.

The goal of education is to equip the child to function as a productive citizen in society. Thus a primary responsibility of parenting is participating in their child's education. There are five goals parents must expect formal education to accomplish: (1) develop the intellectual potential of the child to its fullest; (2) equip the child with marketable skills; (3) contribute to the social development of the child; (4) contribute to the child's appreciation of heritage and community; and (5) develop the child's awareness of humanity.

I am a product of a Southern segregated educational system. All of my public school education and a significant portion of my posthigh school education was in a segregated context. In addition I have been involved in the public school and university educational system as the parent of three children. Thus I come to this section with strong opinions about the role of education in parenting.

In the past, the African American parent has put absolute faith in the power of education to equip their children to succeed in life in spite of the oppressive and unequal society in which they would live. The evidence suggests that this confidence in the power of education was good for all black people. The most potent testimony to the power of education to elevate from poverty to significant success are the Colin Powell's and the Jesse Jackson's of our day. There are many others who could also be mentioned.

However, historically speaking the African American parent did not leave the education of their children to the segregated and biased institutions of their day. Our parents proved themselves to be in partnership with God, the educational institutions, and the community. The common goal of this partnership was to produce an African American adult who was equipped to take his/her place in society and rise to the top of it. It is important to note at this point that the objective of the parents of that day was not to grow adults who could make a lot of money, even though making money was definitely an objective of education; but the primary goal was to grow an adult who would become a significant part of society.

The parents, teachers and community people of that day would say such things as, "You are going to be somebody someday. Just keep on trying to make it." They would also say, "You are going to have something someday; just keep on working hard." The idea of becoming somebody was a reference to the child's potential for intellectual development. The reference to having something was a reference to the child's will to work and do a good job. These two ideas were not necessarily combined in one person, but both were important. You see, in the minds of our forefathers the black community needed both men and women who could contribute to the community through their intellect and also who could contribute to the community economically.

The African American parent must realize that the partnership of years past between the parent, God, and the community does not exist today. Spiritually speaking, the black community lives in spiritual bankruptcy. The social, economic, and educational aspect of the community is infested with the stench of decay today. Thus parents today face the challenge of largely educating their children alone.

I have previously mentioned the spiritual bankruptcy prevalent in the African American community. Many African American parents today are first generation evangelical Christians. Thus it is not wise to assume that church membership and religious involvement are sufficient Christian education for children. The local schools, whether public or private, are hardly equipped to partner with parents in educating children. Perhaps the least prepared of all in terms of partnering with parents in educating children is the black community.

The African American parent needs to determine for themselves the educational goals of each of their children. This education must begin with a sound and thorough Christian education. Then the parents must consider what it is that God will likely do with the child he or she reaches adulthood. With these two decision in view the parent must proceed to find the educational context that will best develop the child according to those goals.

The first fifteen years of my marriage were spent in institutions of higher learning piecing together a solid educational foundation with the fragments of education I had acquired as an African American male in a segregated society. There came a point in my pursuit of higher education that I had to decide to put aside my personal educational goals and give exclusive attention to the education of my children. It was not possible for me to hold a full-time job, be a husband and a father, and also properly educate my children. My wife came to the same conclusion, namely that involvement in the education of the children had to take priority over her personal educational goals.

As a result of our decision to put our educational goals on hold until we educated our children, two of our children graduated from college and the third is a senior in high school. I am not suggesting that we could not have done both successfully. I am simply suggesting that in terms of the education of children the parents do well to make it the top priority.

Involvement in the education of our children not only impacted our personal educational goals, it also impacted our family income. In order to have the freedom to be involved in the education of our children, my wife and I decided that she would only work when the job was such that it did not limit her availability to the children. This meant having less money and often more debt, but it was the right decision for us.

I cannot take credit for being extensively involved in the education of my children on a daily basis, this credit goes to my wife. The educational success of my children is due primarily to the tireless and sacrificial efforts of my wife. Understand that from our point of view, as parents of black children, we had few, if any, partners other than our Lord and Savior, Jesus Christ.

Chapter 15

THE ROLE OF THE EXTENDED FAMILY

The extended family includes the families of both parents of the children. Specifically it may include two sets of grandparents, two sets of aunts, uncles and also cousins. The fact is every child has an extended family. The unfortunate reality is that far too many children know nothing of the family tree of which they are a part.

I once read a button worn by a teenage girl which read, "I am looking for myself. Have you seen me?" So many children, youth, and even adults have no idea of who they are in terms of their family background.

There are no small number of reason for this lack of identity with family blood lines today, not the least of which is the way children are conceived. Added to that is the possessiveness of parents as it pertains to their children. The parents who meet and mate and develop a child will most often grow an adult who has no sense of their father's family. There are far too many African American children today who have no earthly idea as to who they are in terms of their family tree. I refer to this tragic situation as "the legacy of sperm—misplaced and ill-planted."

Bill was a man who seemed to have no real sense of himself. Though he was very brilliant intellectually, he lacked any real sense of family and stability. On any given day Bill might be wearing the personality of this or that TV character, mimicking this TV personality or that one.

In conversation with Bill I discovered that he had no sense of who his family was in terms of his father, grandparents, aunts, and uncles.

For a long time I tried to uncover the cause behind the persistent anger of Sherry. She always seemed to be on the defensive and ready to fight about anything. Sherry's husband and friends often complained about her negative attitude. I had always assumed that Sherry grew up in a family where the extended family was present. It happened one day that I asked Sherry about her father. I was unprepared for her response. "I don't know who my Daddy is," she replied. I then began to understand Sherry's problem.

The extended family concept is considered to be a crucial part of the African American family and community. The prevalence of the extended family among African Americans is significantly overstated. In reality, the involvement of the extended family in the parenting of black children is also seriously overstated. In too many cases only one side of the family is known to the child.

The extended family of both parents provides insight into the child's personal identity. They answer the question, "Who am I?" From the physical features and genetic makeup of the child, to the preferred diet and all things in between, the extended family says, "This is who you are."

It is not at all possible for parents to grow healthy adults apart from the extended family because it is the extended family along with the parents who answer the question, "Where do I belong?" It is evident from the epidemic of gangs and the violence that has come with this social evolution, that a growing number of children are ignorant of who they are and where they fit in as a productive part of society. The average gang member is in search of who they are and where they fit in.

The extended family answers the questions, "Who am I?" and "Where do I belong?" by attitudes and acts of affirmation. *First, the extended family affirms the spiritual foundation the parent lays in the Christian education of the child.* It is difficult to teach Christian principles to your own children when their grandparents, aunts, and uncles disregard, denounce, or disregard them themselves.

Second, the extended family affirms the personal identity of the child. Here the grandparents, aunts, and uncles join together in helping the child develop a strong self-concept with which he/she is comfortable.

Third, the extended family affirms the values and priorities the parents set for the child. It is absolutely necessary for children to see Christian values and life priorities played out in the lives of their extended family.

There is a significant need today in the African American community for models of the nuclear family. There is also a great need for children to be given a sense of security. The extended family is uniquely fitted for such roles.

CHAPTER 16

THE ROLE OF THE COMMUNITY

As stated earlier, in the African American community, both socially and economically, there is the stench of decay. The funeral home owners, the lawyers, and the drug dealers seem to be the most prosperous people in the community. There are times when it seems that the African American community is nothing more than a war zone, not unlike many different underdeveloped third world communities. Yet as an African American parent I know full well that this community has a role in the parenting of black children.

The role of the community in parenting African American children is to answer the question, "How do I fit in with society?" Thus there is to be in the community a value system that is reflective of the values of the parents. Such things as work, honesty, humanitarianism, and such that are taught by the parents are to be evident in the lives of the people in the community. The community is to reflect the values of the families that make up that community. To the extent that this is not the case, parenting is all the more difficult.

There is a story of a group of white Christians who, in their attempt to minister to inner-city children, took a number of the children from the streets of the inner-city where they played in the crowded streets, out to the suburbs where there were few people and plenty of space to play. When asked how they enjoyed the trip to the suburbs the children replied, "Boring." "What was the problem?" the confused host inquired. "There were no people out there," replied the children. These children did not have parents who placed a high value on individual space, the community in which they lived reflected their parents' values. In the suburbs, they were out of their comfort zone.

The community is to be a place in which children learn to practice the social skills taught by their parents. Thus it is the responsibility of the community to be a place of opportunity for African American children. To say that such is not the case in the community today is more than an understatement. Tragically, today the African American community is all about survival, not opportunity. In this context it is well to mention the responsibility of the community to provide entertainment for the children. Children need a place in the community to play, entertain, and be entertained. Such an environment must also be safe and provide an opportunity for work.

Finally, the community is to provide religious experiences in a context that is positive and fulfilling. Thus the local church must also be a functional part of community life for the African American child.

Part 4

Preparing for Parenthood

Chapter 17

Understanding the Basic Needs of Children

In parenting I have developed what I call a "wheel of needs" that every child has which must be met by parents. This "wheel of needs" supports the idea that parenting is an adult responsibility not fit for children. It is also evident from this "wheel of needs" that parenting is best done by those adult men and women who are married and who are mature. Fragmented parents will in most instances fragment children thus producing dysfunctional adults.

There are at least eight basic needs that every child has. These are (1) love and affection; (2) spiritual nurture; (3) positive life values; (4) education; (5) discipline; (6) positive communication; (7) life goals; and 8) security.

In thinking through the basic needs of children, I am reminded of the fact that there are at least three major conspiracies prevalent in our day that are an assault on the institution of parenting. These conspiracies include, but are not limited to, homosexuality, abortion, and abuse. I mention these conspiracies here as a prelude to coming to grips with the basic needs of children.

Every parent must keep in mind that no matter how popular homosexuality becomes it is and has always been inherently evil and an affront to the whole institution of parenting idea as God set it up. To the family, male and female homosexuality represents death in its most final form because it cannot represent fertility and reproduction. It is still perceived socially as a form of sexual perversion. In conversation with an associate of mine, I mentioned that my son was at the age where girls were his top priority. My associate responded by saying, "That's good." I responded by saying, "You mean, that's good because he could be discovering boys?" In these days it is a blessing to have children that are attracted to the opposite sex.

The second major conspiracy against parenting is abortion. Psalm 139:13 says, "For thou didst form my inward parts; thou didst weave me in my mothers womb." The abortionist says the issue is a question of when the unborn becomes a human being as opposed to just a mass of tissue. The Bible identifies that which the abortionist refers to as tissue and counts the trimesters to personhood as a human being whom God is weaving in the womb of the mother. Increasingly it seems as if abortion is becoming the number one alternative to the God-ordained reproductive process. The tools of an abortionist are to the modern day unborn child what Adolph Hitler's gas chambers were for the Jew in the 1940s and what the slaveships were to the Africans in the 1600-1800s. I am convinced that the needs of children must be understood before conception.

There are many conspiracies against parenting God's style—homosexuality and abortion are two of the major ones. To speak to the issue of the basic needs of children without addressing these conspiracies is futile at best, for at the heart of the issue of homosexuality and abortion is the issue of parenting.

When I see the undeveloped corpses of unborn children filling the trash dumpsters outside clinics and hospitals, I am compelled to pose the question, "Whatever happened to motherhood? Did somebody kill her off or did she feel so abased and neglected that she left on her own?"

While it cannot be argued that maternalism is instinctive with women, and on a national average more women kill their children than do men, it can be argued that in terms of understanding the basic needs of children motherhood is paramount.

Increasingly there are cases that occur in which a brutal man, posing as the lover of a woman who has children, has beat to death (or otherwise brutalized) the woman's children. When I hear that a mother has become so starved for affection and so desperate for the attention of a man that she abandons her children to this cruelty, I am compelled to demand an answer to the question, "What ever happened to motherhood? Did she go on strike in protest against being neglected by her subjects?"

We have a serious crisis on our hands as it pertains to fathering. The absentee father is a major social problem today. However, to understand the basic need of children, it must begin with a biblical view of motherhood.

Preaching to the Wind: Whatever Happened to Motherhood?

I return to my earlier example of motherhood. Exodus chapter 2 begins the history of the life of Moses, the great leader who led the Jewish people out of slavery in Egypt. In this text, as it pertained to what God was doing with and in the life of Moses, all of the primary players were women.

The women included the midwives who chose not to obey the edict of the Pharaoh and kill Moses at his birth because he was a Jewish boy. Then there was Moses' mother Jochebed who hid him for three months. Third, there was the daughter of Pharaoh who adopted Moses and raised him as her own son. Finally, there was Miriam, Moses' sister who, when asked by Pharaoh's daughter to find a woman to nurse Moses, got his real mother.

It is important in terms of understanding the basic needs of children to note that God created Moses in the womb of his mother during the time when the government had legalized the infanticide of all Jewish boys. The issue however, was not what the government mandated, but how much of a priority Moses' mother put on mothering. Motherhood can be defined as caring for children according to the basic needs of each child.

In the social and family context of our day, the African American community is caught in the throes of a serious crisis. The government and legal system, along with much of the education system, has issued an unofficial edict that black boys will be destroyed by some means in their early childhood. In this crisis, African American mothers seem to have entered a conspiracy with these systems in destroying black boys. The abortionist's tools are all too often a part of the cycle of violence perpetuated upon black children. The language of women today is commonly filled with unwanted pregnancy statements. It's better to have an abortion than to bring an unwanted child into the world and then abuse it. It may well be that such conspiracies and statements are in fact a reflection of genuine motherhood. However, in many ways, at least in terms of parenting children from the perspective of their basic early childhood needs, motherhood is much more determinative than is fatherhood.

The issue of motherhood must be viewed in the context of the modern-day independent, liberated woman. For a growing number of women, motherhood has lost most of its attractiveness in favor of independence and vocational success. Nine months of pregnancy and the physical limitations that most often accompany it, combined with three to five years of early childhood development, is, in the opinion of a growing number of women, too much of a sacrifice. When motherhood is defined as inherently filled with different kinds of struggles and challenges, a number of women today opt out of it.

In the African American community being a mother is close to the most difficult task a woman could possibly have. The months of pregnancy, the pain of childbirth, and then caring for infants and children is enough to drive any one woman insane. When viewed through the window of its inherent difficulty, one can understand why some women decide against becoming a mother.

When Pharaoh's daughter gave Moses to his mother to nurse until he was weaned, she took him back home and kept him three years until he was weaned. God gave Moses' mother the privilege of providing the early childhood development of her son. From this sovereign act of God it can be concluded that when a mother chooses to invest the time and the sacrifice necessary to mother her children, God will pay high dividends in return.

It is important to note that Moses spent the first three years of his life with his own mother among his own people. When Moses was weaned, his mother, in accordance with the agreement she made, took him up to the palace of the Pharaoh and gave him over to the daughter of the Pharaoh to be raised as her own son. During the thirty-seven years in the house of the Pharaoh's daughter, he was given a thorough Egyptian education, so much so that he dressed, spoke, ate, and acted like an Egyptian. After all of

UNDERSTANDING THE BASIC NEEDS OF CHILDREN

this Egyptian culture and assimilation, it entered the mind of Moses that he was not an Egyptian and he decided to return home to his people (Acts 7:23-24). He even refused to be called the son of Pharaoh's daughter choosing rather to endure ill-treatment with the people of God rather than enjoy the passing pleasures of sin (Heb. 11:24). The motivating force behind all of this was the mothering of his mother during the first three years of his life. It is important to note that in terms of power and influence a mother can accomplish in her children in the early years of their lives what no amount of contrary training can eliminate.

THE BASIC NEEDS OF CHILDREN

The number one basic need of children is love and affection. This love and affection should be provided by both parents but it is especially needed by the mother. Mary, the mother of Jesus, is a excellent example of the significance of motherhood. Keep in mind that Jesus was not born into nor did he grow up in an ideal family situation. He was raised by his stepfather and his mother was accused of being an immoral woman after her impregnation. Yet Mary, like the mother of Moses, was in partnership with God in her mothering. She parented with a purpose, bearing whatever shame she needed to, keeping in mind the things that only she and God knew. Both Mary and Jochebed experienced the joy of seeing their sons exalted.

The second basic need children have is spiritual nurture. The mother is usually the primary teacher in the first three to five years of a child's life. The father's involvement during these years is important as a supportive role with the mother, sharing her and the child's love and affection. This phase is followed by an increasing shift in the role of the father in the parenting. Beginning in the fourth or fifth year the father begins to move into the primary teaching role as the spiritual leader in the home.

The African American father may have learned a method of parenting his sons that is inherently destructive in that it turns them into an angry children who grow into angry men. A few years back a commercial appeared about Michael Jordan which said "I want to be like Mike." Well, when was the last time you heard the son of a black father say, "I want to be like my dad?"

PARENTING IN THE CONTEXT OF A SPIRITUAL DEFICIT

Black men are not the only fathers who have sons who are filled with anger and have lost heart but there does seem to have more than a fair share of such sons in the black community.

There is an alternative to growing angry sons. Note the text in Ephesians 6:4b: "But bring them up in the nurture and instruction of the Lord." When it comes to bring up our children in the nurture and admonition of the Lord I contend that there is a spiritual deficit in the environment of many of our homes which is ultimately reflected in our children. In Proverbs 4:3, Solomon says that in his home the environment was such that he felt like a son to his father. Remember, Solomon's father was King David, Israel's greatest king. David fought more wars, took more land, and expanded the boundaries of the nation of the Jews more than any other king. Yet while doing all of this and managing the affairs of the kingdom of Israel, David took the time to make his son feel like a son.

It is possible to have a family that is well-fed, well-housed and well-clothed and yet have a home in which there is a serious spiritual deficit in the environment. In such a home environment, is it not possible to teach children wisdom. Wisdom is the ability to know the difference between that which seem to be important but is not and that which seems to be important and really is.

This ability to live skillfully, distinguishing between what is important and what is not, is passed from father to son and from heart to heart, not just head to head. The focus is not on being smart but on being wise. To pass wisdom from heart to heart there must be a home environment in which hearts are more evident than heads, and feelings are stronger than attitudes. This is what is means for father's to bring up their children in the nurture and admonition of the Lord.

The parenting of children in the nurture and admonition of the Lord demands a mother who knows how to mother. Look again at Proverbs 4:3b and notice that Solomon says that his mother treated him as if he was her only child; "tender and the only son in the sight of my mother, then he (my father) taught me and said to, "Lyour heart hold fast my words; keep my commandments and live." It was the mother who set this environment in the home.

UNDERSTANDING THE BASIC NEEDS OF CHILDREN

All of the current evidence on parenting in America today supports the conclusion that most of the parenting is done by mothers. However as I understand Proverbs 4:3b, I am convinced that the children who are best equipped to make wise choices in life are those children who are parented well by their father.

Solomon said that his mother set the tone for the environment in the home and when that environment was conducive to being taught, his father taught him. Every son must have a father who teaches him how to carve out for himself a whole and healthy life.

Nurture is more important and more determinative in the kind of adult children grow into than is the social environment in which children grow up in or the genetic blood line of the child. Thus the role of the father as one who nurtures his children is very important.

The third basic need of children is constructive life values. These values are, for the most part, caught by the child and absorbed from the atmosphere of the home. The primary communicator of life values for most children is the father. In terms of life values most of our children catch from the home environment the idea that money is the most important and most valuable thing anybody can get their hands on, even though they may have no idea what to do with it. An illustration may help.

During the story time for children in the Sunday morning worship I told the story of the feeding of the five thousand with the two fish and five loaves of bread. I asked the children that if they had been the one with the fish and bread, would they have given it to Jesus to feed the five thousand. Most of them responded with a resounding, "Yes!" I then asked them if they had a peanut butter and jelly sandwich, would they share it with me and my family. They said, "Yes." However, when I asked those same little children that if they had a dollar would they give it to me, without any hesitation they all shouted, "NO!"

In Proverbs 4, Solomon says we are to acquire wisdom and understanding. The command is to acquire it because no child is born with wisdom. Wisdom is the ability to distinguish between that which seems to be important and is not and that which seems to be important and really is. Wisdom is a positive life value that must be taught and cultivated in children.

Parenting in the Context of a Spiritual Deficit

There is no question that parents today are saying to their children in both word and action, acquire money and more money. What parents have failed to comprehend is the fact that he who has money but lacks an understanding of life is destined to misuse and even lose their money. The truth of this statement is evident in the number of black professional athletes who earn millions of dollars but retire with nothing. It may be that these young men and women have no understanding of the value of a dollar because they have no understanding of life in terms of constructive life values. Thus by the time they discover what life is about, their money and their career is all gone.

In Proverbs I call attention to what wisdom promises to do for those who love her and are devoted and loyal to her, namely, guard and watch over them. This is exactly the same as what we seem to be teaching our children that money will do for them, namely insure their safety and success in life. In the minds of some parents, money has the ability to impart wisdom. But such is not the case.

Wisdom, unlike money, has the power to guard and protect those who love it. Wisdom has the power to direct the life choices of the child by establishing in the child a value system that is built on godliness. A godly value system has the ability to enable a child to see more than what is readily evident, feel more than what is touching them, and sense more than what is verbally expressed. In other words, wisdom imparts functional survival skills. A wise person can look back at yesterday and get some sense of today and can look at today and make some sense of tomorrow. Wisdom is not about being smart or crafty—it is about being transparent and open.

To appreciate the value of a dollar a child must learn the value of life. In Luke 15 is the story of the prodigal son who did not understand the value of a dollar because he had yet to understand the value of life. Thus having left home with all of his inheritance and having randomly spent it he found himself eating hog food in a hog pen. It was in this context that this young man began to understand the meaning of life and the value of a dollar.

The fourth basic need children have is education. While attending a testimony service I was reminded of the need that every child has for a functional education. In this meeting a young man about eighteen years old stood to give his testimony. While standing, he decided to read a passage from the Bible. As I listen to this young man try to read from the Bible, it was clear that while he had the courage to stand before the congregation and read, he lacked the ability to read. I thought, here is a young eighteen-year-old black man who is in effect already not going to succeed in today's society unless he learns to read.

As a parent it must be understood that education is not an option for children. There is no positive place in this world for functionally illiterate people. Thus such people inevitably find themselves in prison or in dead-end jobs.

The first thing parents must understand in order to raise functionally literate people prepared for post-high school education is that they are the primary educators of their children. The public or private school systems are consequently partners in the overall educational endeavor. It is the parents' (not the teachers') responsibility to oversee their children's intellectual and academic development. The primary objective should be for the child to acquire basic reading, writing, arithmetic, and scientific skills which are needed to survive in this technologically advanced society.

Second, parents must be abreast of their children's abilities and limitations. Unfortunately, in many cases, black males are placed into special education classes for reasons other than medical or cognitive deficits. Often, teachers apply stereotypical ideas to black males. Therefore, if no medical or cognitive deficit has been substantiated, parents must make sure their children are not stereotypically placed into special education classes.

While monitoring and educating children, parents must understand that in today's society, with technology advancing daily, a child cannot view high school as an end to his or her education. Continuing education cannot be an option. It is my belief that by the time a child reaches high school, the fact that that child will be continuing the educational process should have long been established. The issue now should be what form of continued education will the child pursue (i.e., college, vocational or technical training, etc.) and what will be the chosen field of study. The idea that some children are not equipped for post-high school education could also be construed as saying some children are not equipped to succeed in life.

Third, African American parents must be prepared to invest financially in the continued education of their child. This means being willing to make whatever sacrifice is necessary to finance that education.

College is a choice that should be made together by both the parent and the child. College is the child's first taste of complete pseudo-independence (pseudo in that although children have free reign to do what they please, most often they are financially dependent on their parents). It is in this context that many children experience their first real failures. Along with all the pressures to fit in and be a part of society, the child reared by Christian parents often comes face to face with the reality of the "real world." Along with this rude awakening, the child must make life long choices regarding career and, many times, mates.

The choice to go to college is one that affects and shapes the rest of the child's life so it is not to be taken lightly. However, it is a decision that should be made with the knowledge of the child's academic capabilities and desire to achieve. I am not saying that every child is not capable of going to college or graduating from a university. The question is, however, does every child have the same desire to succeed.

Dale and Diane have twin boys—Albert and Alvin. Albert had always been an excellent student, putting little effort toward school. Alvin had always had trouble with school, but he expended a great deal of effort to do well and got mostly C's. Both went off to college. Dale and Diane thought that Albert would graduate and they worried about Alvin's progress. However, Alvin graduated in five years while Albert became bored with college and decided to start his own business.

The above example shows that, although academic ability plays a part in a student's ability to progress at the college level, discipline and desire go a lot further.

To say that education is a basic need of children is to say that there is no possible means of real survival in this country without a functional education. The content and focus of the education of black children must be such that it prepares them to compete first in the American job market, and second in the world job market. For the African American parent this means being unwilling to endorse athletics as the all-sufficient vocation for their sons and daughters. Children must be equipped intellectually, emotionally, morally, and socially to function in the twenty-first century.

The fifth basic need of children is discipline. Recently in a shopping mall on the south side of Dallas, two teenage black boys were caught by a few men from the Nation of Islam burglarizing a store. The men from the Nation of Islam took the boys and whipped them in the nude. The City of Dallas arrested the men for whipping the boys.

However the response of the black community was quite interesting in that, for some, the action of the men was consistent with the tradition of parenting in the black community, while for others, such action by the men was nothing short of criminal. Ultimately the men were released without charge. These boys, judging from the scars they had from the caning, would be unlikely to go out and burglarize another business in the future.

At the center of the issue of the caning of these two teenage boys was the issue of discipline. Historically the African American parent has been strong on discipline when it came to their children. The idea of discipline was in fact a community responsibility.

In my trips to Israel I most often go down to the Wailing Wall and observe the Jewish bar mitzvah. This is a ceremony that comprises a Jewish father and his son. The mother is excluded. The ceremony takes place when the Jewish boy reaches the age of twelve and it signals the beginning of the coming together of the boys mind, muscles, and heart. In other words, it is about discipline. It seems that orthodox Judaism places a priority on discipline.

As I have traveled abroad it is clear that most countries view discipline as a basic need of children. Yet in America, this is no longer the case. The African American parent has lost sight of the need children have to be disciplined. The Scriptures are replete with verses on the value of discipline in growing children. Examples include: "The rod and reproof give wisdom, but a child who gets his own way brings shame to his mother" (Prov. 29:15); "Foolishness is bound up in the heart of a child; The rod of discipline will remove it far from him" (Prov. 22:15); and "Do not hold back discipline from the child, although you beat him with the rod, he will not die" (Prov. 23:13).

PARENTING IN THE CONTEXT OF A SPIRITUAL DEFICIT

There are three valuable results that Scripture promises as a result of discipline. The method of discipline includes both corporal punishment and verbal admonition. Parents who are constant in their discipline will find that the child will gain wisdom which gives them the ability to live skillfully.

The parent who disciplines their children will drive from their hearts the spirit of delinquency that accompanies the early years of the child's life. Without consistent discipline the child will grow into adulthood with this spirit of delinquency still very much in tact.

The parent who consistently discipline their children will save their lives as adults. Proverbs 23:13 says in effect that effective discipline rids the child of attitudes and behavior that, if maintained into adulthood, will likely cost the child his/her life.

To speak of corporal punishment in this day is to risk being classified as one who agrees with abusing children. However one must consider what the scriptures teach regarding the discipline of children. It is clear to me that discipline must include corporal punishment, not to it's exclusion, but it also must include a variety of methods. However, the goal must be the same for each child. That goal is best summarized in Proverbs 17:6: "Grandchildren are the crown of old men, and the glory of sons is their fathers." Christian parents must take seriously the admonition of the Bible in disciplining their children.

The sixth basic need children have is positive communication. From time to time I, along with many others, involve myself in the ongoing dialog about the issue of nature versus nurture. There are those today who, like the authors of the book, *The Bell Curve* and *The End of Racism* that contend that black people in general and men in particular are intellectually deficient and violently inclined because of their basic nature. To say the least, such views lack any substance, scientific or otherwise.

Positive thinking and positive adults, no matter their race or culture, are the result of the positive environment in which they grew up. The very foundation of a positive home environment in the ability and the will to communicate consistently in a positive, non-threatening, non-critical and non-judgmental manner.

Cheneiqua had no concept of her beauty. In fact she

felt that she was neither attractive or smart. I asked her what she saw when she looked into the mirror. Her response surprised me. She said she saw a very ugly, dumb woman. I told her that since she was obviously not unattractive, from what source did she get the idea that she was ugly and dumb. She said she had gotten the idea from her parents.

Cheneiqua's parents most likely did not sit down with her and tell her she was ugly and dumb. No, her parents most likely created a negative home environment in which the mood, words, and the attitudes were ugly and non-affirming. What Cheneiqua learned to believe about herself was learned from her home environment.

Keyshun grew up in a single parent home in which he was the darling of his mother's life. She constantly raved about how good-looking he was. Yet when Keyshun blossomed into a young man he was negative and prone to violence. In this case the mother's positive attitude towards her son was overruled by the mother's negative attitude towards most other people in general, and towards Keyshun's father in particular.

Positive communication is a basic need of every child for out of the soil of communication each child must shape for themselves a self-concept that will last their whole lifetime. Thus the environment of the home must be one where vocabulary fills the air with positive affirmation and encouragement. Anything less will warp the child's self-image.

As a young boy my head was the largest part of my body, thus I was repeatedly referred to as a "big head water head nigger." I was not one given to fighting but these words would incite me to anger and I would fight. As I reflect on that experience as a young boy I can still feel the rage that incited in me. Positive communication is a basic need that all children have.

Life goals are the seventh basic need that children have. This means children ought not be the product of their parents having fun, though one would not want to deny the inherent pleasure of sex. However, children ought to be developed from the point of view that they are the product of the personal and intentional hand of the living God and because they are.

A young Christian woman shared her testimony with

me in which she said that she was the product of lust and sin on the part of her parents. As I listened to this testimony I thought how sad it was for such a thing to have happened. The thing I found so sad was the fact that this young woman grew up in a world in which she did not know that, even though her parents might not have conceived her in love, she is nonetheless the product of the creative hand of the living God. The fact that she was the product of the creative powers of the living God meant that God had a plan for her life. It was the absence of this knowledge that contributed to the wasteful and sinful life this young woman lived for many years.

In terms of life goals children need to know that God is their creator and parents need to see themselves as partners with God in the parenting process. With this combination both the parent and the child will have life goals that have an eternal perspective on life. An eternal perspective on life allows both the parent and the child to look beyond present circumstances no matter the nature of the circumstances to a tomorrow in which things will be different. Thus such things as immediate self gratification are less of a problem to the child. Failure in some areas is not viewed as such a traumatic problem when the goal is tempered with an eternal perspective.

Parents who equip their children with positive life goal must themselves be equipped with such goals. The parent who lives life as if there is no tomorrow will likely not be able to develop positive life goals in their children. A life that has positive life goals not only is tempered with an eternal perspective but it has a strong commitment to a Christian agenda. Such parents model the idea of investing oneself in service to the Lord Jesus Christ. Let me be specific here. Parents who give their children positive life goals are parents who model such things as discipline, humility, moderation, hope, forgiveness, good stewardship of their time and resources, and a strong work ethic.

My father was a model of a man who highly valued education. Yet my Dad was functionally illiterate. His model of the value of education was evident in the value he placed on our getting an education. In the mind of my father there was no reason good enough to surface for my not being in school. Neither my health, the weather, work, nor fear of being beat up was sufficient reason for me to miss school.

In addition there was no excuse for flunking a class. My father believed that if the subject could be taught then I could learn it. There was no such thing as not being able to understand the teacher. My father included education as one of my life goals, I have never abandoned that goal.

Finally my father and mother modeled a strong work ethic and, to this very day I have been hooked on work. In addition, my mother did a great job of sharing what she had with others. She demonstrated the value of living life with an eternal perspective in view. It was this model of selflessness that no doubt shaped my spirit for a lifetime of pastoral ministry.

The modern day African American parent must understand that it is not enough to work hard and provide all the material things that children need. Strong consideration and effort must be put forth to develop in children positive life goals. These life goals must be evident in the parent.

The eighth basic need that children have is a need for security. Security for children means living in what I call a non-threatening environment. This is the kind of environment in which the parents make sure that the basic needs of health, food, clothing, and shelter are consistently met. In addition, and perhaps even more important, the parent must provide for the children an environment in which there is consistent emotional security. The strongest and most consistent provision of security parents can provide is their evident love for and commitment to each other. Parents who fight, separate, and otherwise abuse each other will most often cause their children to feel insecure.

When my children were small, and even now as adults, when they discover that their mother and I are upset with each other about something they each begin to intercede with us on behalf of the other. They will try to get us to start talking to each other or do something to help us to make up. The idea that their parents might not be happy together is quite unsettling to them. I think such is the case with most children. The best demonstration of love parent can show towards their children is their love for each other.

CHAPTER 18

PARENTING FROM THE BACK OF A HEARSE

On Sunday evening October 25, 1970 the congregation of Bibleway Church met for Bible study. Following the study I dismissed the congregation and stood talking as usual to various members. Suddenly a teenage boy approached me carrying my seven year old and only son, Kenneth, in his arms. As the young man approached me he said rather solemnly, "Pastor! Something has happened to Kenneth! He was chasing another little boy across the parking lot and he fell and did not get up!" As I reached out to take my seven-year-old into my arms I quickly realized that something was seriously wrong with him. His body was limp and his breathing was shallow. I quickly headed to the hospital emergency room. Halfway to the hospital my only son took a deep breath and died in my arms. A few minutes later we arrived at the hospital and he was officially pronounced dead. The autopsy showed that he had developed a rare heart disease that caused his heart to suddenly stop beating as he chased his little friend across the church parking lot.

At the time I was the senior pastor of Bibleway Bible Church and a second-year seminary student. For the first time in my life I was faced with a side of parenting I was totally unprepared to deal with. In my mind, parenting up to that point was all about life and development. It was about learning how to shape character and grow a healthy adult. Yet I was faced with the impossible task of demonstrating how to "parent from the back of a hearse."

I think it would have been different had it been that our son would have shown some symptoms of a bad heart but such was not the case. He was born healthy and his pediatrician never discovered anything wrong with his heart. As far as we knew, until the moment we got the autopsy report, our firstborn was completely healthy. He was not supposed to die but he did. His death was sudden and traumatic.

As parents the sudden unexpected death of our son raised a multitude of troubling and unsettling questions in our mind like "Were we good parents? Should we have know something was wrong? Did we provide him with the best medical care possible?" Those and a host of other difficult questions filled our minds.

As Christian parents we faced more questions such as "What did we do wrong to deserve such an experience? Why did God give us a son only to take him so soon? Did not God know that children are not supposed to die?"

As a pastor I faced still other questions, such as "How do we grieve? Who will do the funeral? What do we say to the congregation?" A major question was "Where do we go to find the answer to why this happened to us?"

As I reflect on that experience I recognize that just as there is joy in the heart of parents when a child is born, when a child dies it is just as fitting for a father and mother to cry. I recall quite clearly a fellow clergyman saying to me "Do you think it is fitting before God for you to cry like this? Why not accept the will of God and go on?" I said to that brother, "I cannot imagine that God does not understand my broken and grieving heart over the death of my son." The first principle I suggest to parents who must parent from the back of a hearse is that it is OK for both the mother and the father to cry. In fact I think the death of a child demands the shedding of tears.

The second principle is to anticipate and receive the comforting of your grieving heart by God the Holy Spirit. This means being able and willing to encourage yourself in the Lord. I discovered in my grief as a parent who was also a pastor that the congregation had no idea what to say to comfort me. Those who came by during that time most often said nothing. One member said to me, "Pastor, could it be that God is punishing you for some secret sin in your life?" The point was why would God do such a tragic thing if you are as good as you claim to be.

The third principle is to be careful not to ask God why. He will not answer that question. Besides you must understand that there is no satisfactory answer to that question. In this same vein, the parent whose child dies must refuse to blame God for depriving them of their child.

The experience of parenting from the back of a hearse is not one from which there is immediate recovery. In fact, in our case neither Betty nor I have recovered from the death of our son Kenneth, even though it has been over twenty-five years ago.

The death of our firstborn, though tragic and heartbreaking, made a major positive contribution to our family, namely we have two additional children, our daughter Carla and our son Eddie II, who most likely would not have been born had Kenneth not died.

In this vein, when I say to people that we have three living children they immediately respond by saying, "Oh, good planning and timing!" Such is not the case at all. When Kenneth died in a moment we went from what we considered to be an ideal family of two children—a girl and a boy with the boy being the oldest—to a one child family with a three year old girl who was had been thoroughly traumatized by the sudden loss of her brother.

The trauma that our daughter experienced following the death of her brother evidenced itself in an inability to sleep. Each night she would have horrifying nightmares that sent her into hysteria night after night. It was in this situation that Betty and I turned to the Lord and prayed for another child. Three years after the death of our first born God answered our prayer and gave us a beautiful daughter. The birth of this daughter brought an end to the horrifying nightmares that our oldest daughter was experiencing.

During the early years of our second daughter's life her sister told her everything she remembered about her brother so that it is possible for our second daughter to speak as much about her oldest brother whom she never saw as can her sister. It happened that our two daughters decided that they wanted a brother and they turned to God in prayer and asked God to give them a brother. Six years after the birth of our second daughter, God answered her prayer and gave Betty and I a second son and our daughters a second brother.

I must confess that I was totally unconvinced that God would answer their prayers for a brother but our daughters were so convinced that He would that they chose his name even before their mother got pregnant. I remained unconvinced up until our son was delivered.

Thus, the fact that our children are all six years apart is not our arrangement—it is God's arrangement. It keeps us mindful of a number of things, not the least of which is that children are a heritage from the Lord.

Part 5

The Parenting Process

Chapter 19

Preparing the Nest

Premarital counseling is a must for those who plan to establish a Christian home. In this counseling the counselor should include time discussing the parenting process with the couple. The focus in this counseling is to bring the couple to the point where they see parenting as a crucial part of the family life but not the whole of it. Thus parenting that is well-planned is the best way to parent.

The ideas and concepts set forth in this section are consistent with the biblical ideal on how to launch a successful marriage. This means that the concepts suggested here are not reflective of naiveté but rather a reflection of my understanding of and commitment to the biblical idea of how a couple should begin their married life.

The Old Testament sets forth the idea that a couple who marries should have a year together without any major commitments like the husband having to go off to war and such. The point is that in an ideal situation a newly wedded couple would have a year that was specifically given to their bonding together emotionally, spiritually, sexually, and socially. What a great idea.

Though it is hardly possible today for a couple to have the option to experience such a blissful first year of marriage, it is possible for a couple to delay their entrance into the parenting process. I suggest to newlyweds that they delay their parenting at least two years into their marriage. What happens in the first two years of marriage is crucial in determining how well the couple will parent.

PARENTING IN THE CONTEXT OF A SPIRITUAL DEFICIT

The first two years of marriage without pregnancy is "foundation building time." During this time the couple establishes their love for each other based on the reality of who they are as individuals. This involves moving from the imaginary ideas of who each one is in the eyes of the other to the reality of who each one really is. Then they move on to who they are together as husband and wife.

This transition from the ideal to the real thing is most important in beginning the bonding process between the newly married couple. A child conceived during the foundational building time is likely to be viewed by the husband as an intrusion into his world of love and romance with his wife. In addition, pregnancy and the subsequent birth of a child permanently change the relationship between the couple. The wife diminishes her focus on being a bride and increases her focus on motherhood.

The arrival of the first child tends to alter the attitude of the wife towards her husband in that she will naturally give the baby what may appear to be a disproportionate portion of her time. The attitude of the husband towards the wife may also be altered especially in the areas of romance and sex. This changed attitude in the husband often reflects his resentment towards the baby who has replaced him as the number one attention-getter in the home.

The stress of pregnancy and parenting can break a newly-formed marriage, especially when the couple has not had the time to bond together. In addition, the pregnant wife experiences a multitude of biological and emotional changes including gaining weight. This too can affect the attitude of the husband towards his wife. It is my contention that the very nature of childbearing demands time to build a foundation in the marriage relationship that is capable of sustaining the parenting process.

I remember well the excitement of John and Brenda when they got married a few years ago. They had a brief but exciting honeymoon and they both returned to their jobs and began the routine life of a young married couple.

In the first two years of their marriage John and Brenda had two children. As I observed them together it was clear to me that the arrival of the children had seriously altered their relationship. John was as he had always been tall, slim, neat, and handsome. Brenda, on the other hand, was seriously overweight, tired, and not

PREPARING THE NEST

neatly dressed. The fact is Brenda was not physically or emotionally the same young woman that John had married. Although John was a serious Christian he was increasingly dissatisfied with the wife of his youth (Prov. 5).

It is the opinion of some that parenting is the primary function of Christian couples. Thus the argument is made that parenting should take priority over such things as romance, sexuality, entertainment, and other such things in the marriage relationship. I disagree with this view. It is my contention that the primary priority of a marriage should be the couple themselves, not the children. This does not mean that parents should neglect their children. It does mean that parenting should be kept in perspective as a responsibility of those who decide to become parents. The decision to become parents should make an allowance of at least two years of preparation before the parenting process begins and children should be spaced so that the body and mind of the wife has time to recover from the enormous task of having made a human being.

My wife and I were married three and one half years before she conceived our first child. I still recall the nine months she carried our first child with a great degree of horror. I cannot describe the surprise I felt as a young husband as I watched our first pregnancy transform my one hundred and fifteen pound, easy-going, gentle wife into a woman I hardly knew. Halfway through that first pregnancy I swore before God we would never participate in this thing again. I was prepared to take a vow of celibacy.

It was very fortunate for Betty and I that we had three and a half years together before we began our parenting. Having married when Betty was twenty and I was twenty-one and being filled with all the passion of youth, the first three years of our marriage without children gave us the necessary time to lay a solid foundation of love and affection for each other before we became parents. This relational foundation building time proved crucial to the core of our many years of happy marriage.

As our children have grown into adulthood, much to my surprise, I have discovered that the love Betty and I have for each other is what causes our children to believe that we love them. It is not so much how we treat our children that makes them know we love them, but it is how we treat each other that makes them believe we love them.

PARENTING IN THE CONTEXT OF A SPIRITUAL DEFICIT

The first time a young man said to me, "I do not want to spend all of my youth raising children," I was angered by both his words and his attitude. For after all, he helped make those babies and in my view it was his responsibility to take care of them, no matter that it meant surrendering the passions of his young adult life to the parenting process. "I do not want to spend all of my young adulthood parenting," the young man said to me, and I despised him for saying what he felt. Yet, his words have stayed with me for many years. What did he mean by what he said? Are these the words of another black man shirking his responsibility and excusing himself for it? Why was he given the children if he did not want to father them?

Time and experience as a pastor and a father have provided some answers to my questions about the young man's statement. I have discovered that while the Bible says that children are a blessing from the Lord and a man who has many of them is blessed (Ps. 127, 128), it is with the wife of his youth that a young man is to rejoice (Prov. 5:18). The wife's body is to excite her husband at all times (Prov. 5:19).

I have concluded therefore that parenting is not to occupy the whole of a young couple's life. Loving each other is to hold that priority in the marriage. I do not think that being married is synonymous with parenting. In my view the best parents are the parents who are lovers first and have each other as their respective priorities.

The first two years of marriage is foundation building time and during this time the couple establishes their love for each other, moving from the imaginary to the reality. They develop a positive environment that is reflective of the love they share for each other. They begin the emotional and overall bonding process that gives birth to their new world and that is reflective of both their worlds.

The final thing that this first two years is to accomplish is the preparation for the second lifelong commitment of parenting. Marriage is itself the first lifelong commitment that a couple enters into—parenting is the second.

I define headship in the Christian home as the ability of a husband to manage his family is a holistic, positive manner. This mean that the man who takes a bride is perceived to have the ability to manage not only himself but a wife as well. Parenting then adds a third dimension to the management responsibility of the husband.

Much is said today about the African American male's neglect in fathering the children he begets. The flip side of the single African American mother is the unemployed African American male. It is in this context that I mention the need for foundation building time in the first two years of marriage for it is in these two years that the African American husband prepares economically for the parenting process.

It is the African American female who is the second highest paid professional in America, not the African-American male. Thus for the African American male the decision to have children can literally dismantle the lifestyle to which he aspires. It can be argued therefore that the African American couple needs time to prepare economically for the parenting process.

Within eleven months after we were married Betty and I purchased our first home. To say the least, we were more than a little bit excited. With the house came the need for new furniture, appliances, and of course a new car. It was right in the middle of paying for all those things that we had purchased to support our chosen lifestyle that Betty got pregnant with our first child. It happened that with the pregnancy came sickness that was related to the pregnancy and Betty had to quit work and stay home. It had never occurred to me that Betty was making twice as much money as I was and then it was gone. Now all the bills were mine to pay.

It was the arrival of our first child that seriously diminished our economic situation and there was nothing I could do about it. Through divine intervention, however, we were able to retain all that we had purchased. It is important to see here that it was the foundation building time that equipped us to weather the storm of this new lifelong commitment of parenting. Our parenting began in 1963. Now it is 1996 and we are still at it—with several years still left.

The first two years of marriage is the foundation building time where the couple establishes their love for each other, develops a positive home environment, begins the bonding process between the two of them, and prepares for the second lifelong commitment of parenting.

CHAPTER 20

CONCEPTION AND BIRTH OF THE FIRST CHILD

While I was in Memphis, Tennessee in May of 1996, I listened with intense interest to the current mayor, who is African American, address the issue of crime in that city. He made mention of the fact that he was particularly interested in the spiraling rate of black on black crime. While crime in general in America is said to be on the decline, according to this mayor, the crime rate in Memphis was high and going higher.

Unfortunately, the problem this mayor is experiencing with black on black crime is a problem all over this country. I cannot help but think that foundational to the issue of black on black crime is the parenting process. There is a deficit in the very fiber of the African American parenting process that must be addressed.

Let me suggest that the thousands of dollars invested in weddings in the African American community be invested instead in the first two years of the couple's marriage. The amount of money invested in a wedding should reflect the economic status of the marrying families, and so should it be with the investment in the first two years of marriage. The goal is to free up the couple so they can have a proper "foundation building time." The conception and birth of the first child is a time of great excitement. This period of time covers the nine months of pregnancy and the first two years of the child's life.

During the nine months of pregnancy the couple is compelled to obtain for the mother and child the very best of prenatal care. Anything less than that is not acceptable. Sufficient health care insurance is a must.

The health management of the pregnant mother must include the whole woman and child. This is physical, spiritual, emotional, and relational. For the husband this means being equipped to nurture the wife with a nest-tending attitude that takes the time to show holistic and whole-hearted care. This is a time when the mobility of the pregnant wife sets the pace for the mobility of the husband. Thus the statement, "We are pregnant," is an accurate statement of this stage of marriage. It is just as accurate as is the statement, "We have a child." The involvement of the husband in the pregnancy phase is all inclusive. This is not a trap the wife makes by herself.

In addition to managing the health care of pregnant wife and child, nurturing the wife, and tending the nest, this is a time in which new attitudes and priorities must be developed. During the pregnancy the physical makeup of the wife's body will likely change significantly. The attitude of the wife towards her appearance will substantially change, many times in a negative way. The conception and birth of the child places a third person into the home. The couple will in short order lose most of the privacy they have experienced together prior to conception and the birth of the first child.

The couple must now adjust to the new roles of parents with all the rights and responsibilities that go with those titles. This means absorbing the economic responsibilities, the emotional demands of a child, the constraining limitations of going out together, and having company.

Sylvia and Richard were enjoying spending time together at home and going out to movies, and occasionally they took a weekend trip to a resort area. When Sylvia got pregnant they, for the most part, continued their established routine with minor adjustments. However, when their first child was born their whole pattern of spending time together and going out suddenly changed and they were forced to stay home and parent their child. For Sylvia and Richard this was not a welcomed experience but one they out of necessity adjusted to.

In parenting the extended family is very valuable

PARENTING IN THE CONTEXT OF A SPIRITUAL DEFICIT

whether that extended family is biological or spiritual. However, the parenting process is the primary responsibility of the birth parents. It is ideal for a couple to have and parent just one set of children. The second generation of children should parent their own children. To put it bluntly, grandparents are poor parents the second time around. Thus parents ought not parent their children's children.

In this second phase I have said that the parenting process includes health care management for the mother and child, the nurturing of the mother and unborn child by the father, developing new attitudes and priorities, and adjusting to new roles and responsibilities.

CHAPTER 21

BUILDING AN ADULT

At this point in the parenting process the couple has been married approximately five years. Two years have been invested in building and securing their own inner personal relational foundation. They are moving successfully from the imaginary to the reality in terms of who each other is. They merge from the two separate worlds they brought together when they married and are being refashioned into a single new world of combined values, ideal, goals , and objectives.

Close to three years have been invested in the conception and birth of their first child. The stress of pregnancy and the birth of the child have passed and this new lifelong commitment of parenting is in process. The third phase of the parenting process covers at least ten years in which the parents are involved in building a foundation inside of the child upon which a whole nonfragmented adult can develop. This ten-year period is divided into two parts, consisting of four years for the first part and six years for the second part. Each part have a specific focus in terms of what is to be accomplished in the child.

Keeping in mind that the parents have invested almost three years in the parenting process, including the conception, pregnancy and birth of the child; this third phase is a continuation of what is already in progress. The focus of the first four of this ten year period is *character shaping.* Shaping the character of the child has in mind teaching the child the meaning of integrity. It involves laying the foundation for the development of the personality of the child. It means giving the child an identity with a positive self-esteem.

It is here that I call attention to the necessity of having built an environment in the home that is conducive to building character that is flavored with a Christian orientation. Proverbs 22:6 says, "Train up a child in the way that it should go and when it is old it will not depart from it." The principle in this passage is this: Create in the child a taste for the good life and time cannot erase that taste. The parent must fashion the character of the child around genuine Christ-centered love.

The prodigal son in Luke 15 is an example of a man who as a child was given a taste of the good life by his father. This taste for a quality life showed up in the man later in life, at a time when he was at his lowest spiritually and economically. In a pigpen, this young man remembered the life he was exposed to as a child and made up his mind to return to that good life. In the mind of this young man, life as a slave in the house of his father was much to be preferred to the life he had succumbed to as a prodigal.

Jimmy was about three years old when he came to the Early Childhood Development Center where I served as Executive Director. On a regular basis Jimmy would go into a rage and attack the teacher and then he would proceed to bite himself so that his teeth prints were deeply embedded in his flesh. No amount of discipline could restrain this destructive behavior in little Jimmy.

Out of desperation Jimmy's teacher brought him to my office and I reached out, pulled him into my arms and hugged him. After a while I said to Jimmy, "What is the matter with you?" "Nothing," Jimmy replied. With a great deal of compassion in my heart for this little boy, I prayed for him, asking the Lord to show me how to help him.

After a little while I felt prompted to ask Jimmy about his parents. "My mother is at home," Jimmy said. "Where is your dad?" I asked Jimmy. "My dad is dead," he replied. "What happened to your dad? How did he die?" "A man shot him and he died," Jimmy said. "How do you know that a man shot your dad?" I asked. "I saw him," Jimmy replied. "You saw the man kill your dad?" I said to Jimmy. "Yes," said Jimmy.

Having heard little Jimmy's story I begin to understand that, at this early age of three, his character had already been flawed by the traumatic environment into which he was born and in which he lived. Children are not emotionally equipped to survive such emotional trauma without serious fragmentation.

This kind of trauma evidences itself later in an unhappy adult. As I worked with both Jack and Jeff, brothers who were both married and in marriage counseling, it became increasingly evident that each of these brothers was flawed in their personalities in that their ability to trust anybody, including their wives, was nonexistent. Lack of trust was just one of their many relational problems.

I inquired into their background and discovered that when these men were boys they experienced the unimaginable horror of watching their father murder their mother in a fit of rage. This traumatic experience at the early age of four and five seriously warped the character of these brothers. Parents must make every effort to develop an environment in the home in which love and affection is so much a part, that the character of the children are infected with that love.

The national problem of teen violence among African Americans is reflective of the negative context in which children are conceived, born, and nurtured. To change the violent behavior of teens we must change the violent environment in which they are nurtured. This means developing a home environment in which love is the prevailing attitude. It is an environment in which hearts are more important than are heads. Feelings are give preference to one's personal agenda.

In character shaping, seeds of integrity, seeds of identity, and seeds of personality and self-esteem are all planted in the spirit of the child. The spirit of the children is like virgin soil and must be nurtured and protected from traumatic experiences. In character shaping, it is essential that the genetic background, and the race and culture of the child be consistent with that of the child. It seems unlikely that the character of a child can be properly developed in a family environment that is different from its race and culture, unless the social context in which the child will live as an adult is not racially prejudiced.

In the book of Exodus chapter 2 is the story of Moses and his mother Jochebed. Moses' mother had only the first three years of her son's life to shape his character, establish his value system, and bend his will. After the first three years of parenting, Moses mother gave him up and, through divine providence, Moses became the adopted son of the daughter of the Pharaoh.

The next thirty-seven years of Moses' life, from age three to forty, was spent in the palace of the Egyptian Pharaoh, where he was educated in all the things of Egyptian culture (Acts 7:22). However, after thirty-seven years of being Egyptianized, at age forty Moses cast aside his Egyptian training and all the prestige that went with being the son of the Pharaoh's daughter and chose to live his life as a Jew, along with all the oppression, persecution and limitations that went with being a Jew in Egypt. This decision by Moses was rooted in the three years of parenting that his mother did before he was turned over to the Pharaoh's daughter to raise.

In the first three years of his life, Moses' mother shaped his character and gave him a God-focus that could not be replaced by all the gods of Egypt. What Moses' mother did with her son in terms of shaping his character was more important than the time she had to do it in.

Parents must be concerned with character building in their children. This means using the time they have, however much or little, to shape the character of the child. What you do is far more important than how much time you have to do it.

Parent must also give attention to planting values in their children during this phase of parenting. This means giving the child a sense of personal significance, and treating the child in such a way that he or she develops a sense of self-worth. This is a time when children need to feel secure and to have a sense of belonging. Teaching values to children is not so much about things you give to the child; it is about how the child is treated as an individual, in words and attitude. For many parents, too much emphasis is placed on giving gifts to the child and too little attention is given to the child as an individual.

Every child needs a home environment in which they are treated special. This means making personal time for each child. Solomon said in Proverbs 4 that he was a son to his father and in the eyes of his mothers he was as an only son. Solomon is saying that his father took the time to give value to him as a son and his mother gave to him such value that he felt as if he was an only child.

While David was king, he took the time to be a father to his son thus giving him value. Lot, on the other hand, is an example of a man who in his value system prioritized prosperity over that which was spiritual. Lot choose to live in an environment that was so evil that it was grievous to his very soul for the sake of material gain. In this environment, Lot's spirit was grieved but the price his wife and children paid was far greater, for they developed a value system that was consistent with the evil of their environment. Lot's values system ultimately led to the destruction of him and his entire family.

As did Lot in biblical days, far too many African American parents today have so prioritized material gain that they cannot take the time to shape the character of their children and plant the seeds of value in them. The middle-class African American tends to pay value to their children with things of high quality, including expensive clothes, cars, and jewelry. What is missing most often in the child is a sense of personal significance, a sense of belonging, a sense of security. For you see, it is not the things you give a child that create character, it is how you treat the child as an individual that creates character.

Betty and I were in the midst of establishing our own middle-class lifestyle when we conceived our first child. As I mentioned earlier, we were in serious debt at the time and my wife was earning the greater part of our household income. The pregnancy was such that she had to quit work and stay home, most often confined to bed. I was left with all the bills and insufficient funds from which to pay them. Somehow we made it through those years without losing anything significant.

However, this experience had the net effect of Betty not working full-time anymore. It is my opinion that the choice we made for Betty to be home with the children, even though we could not afford to do so and maintain our existing lifestyle, is largely responsible for the way our children have turned out as adults. All three children are committed Christians. Two of our three children have finished college and are married. The youngest is a senior in high school. What is most encouraging to Betty and I is the character of our children—they are Christ-focused.

Parenting in the Context of a Spiritual Deficit

There is no substitute for parents being home with children when it comes to establishing values. For some parents the decision to parent in effect means choosing to have less—educationally, materially, and socially. For Betty and I, the decision for her to be home with the children, even though we felt called to full-time Christian ministry, meant delaying the pursuing of both of our goals to acquire educational credentials, economic status, and our spiritual agendas. We chose instead to live and serve with fewer spiritual, social, and economic perks.

I can well remember the times when our friends would boast about their educational attainments, thereby inferring that Betty and I were something less than successful because we were not pursuing the same goals. The fact is we did not share the values of our associates. Today we are still convinced that we made the better choice, and our children attest to the wisdom of that choice.

It is the opinion of some childhood development specialists that the will of children must be broken and then rebuilt in a constructive way. I do not share this view for a number of reasons. I believe that the will of the African-American child is best bent and shaped by the parent rather than being broken by anyone. I am not of the opinion that the children of broken people should have their spirit broken with a view to refashioning it. Parents should bend the will of the child so that it develops positive interpersonal skills and is highly motivated to achieve that which is positive.

Finally this four-year period that is part of this ten-year phase needs to involve the molding of the attitude of children so that they feel good about who they are in terms of their family background, culture, and history. This is the phase in which the parents begin the Deuteronomy 6 kind of teaching about God and his involvement with their parents and their history.

Tony and Marie had two children between the ages of three and five when they came to see me about a problem they were having over celebrating Christmas. Tony was of the opinion that Christmas was not to be celebrated as a Christian holiday with a Christmas tree, lights, etc. Marie did not have a problem with Tony's conviction except when she and the children went home to visit her parents, they and all of her brothers and sisters celebrated Christmas with trees, lights, gifts, food and all the rest. It was the contention of Marie that the difference between how she and Tony celebrated Christmas with their children and how her family celebrated Christmas with their family was a serious problem for their children in that it was difficult for their children to accept the fact that celebrating Christmas that way was wrong when their grandparents and all the aunts, uncles, and cousins did it that way.

The issue of celebrating or not celebrating Christmas is just one of a multitude of concerns the African American parent must be concerned about in terms of the values and convictions that are passed on to their children in the formative years of their lives.

Remember that the Christian African American parents today are parenting in the context of a spiritual deficit. This means that in more than a few instances the extended family does not share the spiritual convictions of the Christian parent. As was true in the case of Tony, Marie and their children regarding how Christmas was to be celebrated, so it it with moral, social, domestic, and economic convictions. To the extent that the extended family differs from what the Bible says, to that extent must the Christian family be concerned about how much influence the extended family is to have in the formative years of their child's life.

Most children at an early age are able to choose from the habits of the extended family members to which they are frequently exposed. These habits may be good or bad. Christian parents must decide to limit the time their children spend with their grandparents when the grandparents do not share the spiritual conviction of the parents.

It is also important to mention here the absolute necessity of parents developing and maintaining a healthy and positive environment in the home. This means making every effort as husband and wife not to be each other's critic in the presence of the children. This means being willing to manage conflict in a non-destructive way for the sake of the children. This means refusing to attack the individual when there is disagreement. This means maintaining an atmosphere in which hearts are more important than are heads.

PARENTING IN THE CONTEXT OF A SPIRITUAL DEFICIT
TROUBLED CHILD EQUALS TROUBLED HOME

Unfortunately, by the age of four or five a number of children are showing signs of becoming seriously fragmented in their character. These children tend to be overly aggressive, negative, and destructive. They tend to have underdeveloped personal identity and are already showing sign of low self-esteem.

These children tend to be violent towards others, both verbally and physically, and they show an interest in sex that is unusual for children that age. In addition they tend to be quite self-sufficient in their ability to take care of themselves. Yet their intellect may be seriously underdeveloped, their creativity stunted and they tend to respond to junk food as real food.

The cause behind the fragmentation in these children can be found in the home from which they came. When the nest into which children are conceived and born is characterized by negativity, destruction, and violence the children from that nest will inevitably be fragmented by the time they reach the age of five.

A few of the troubling characteristics of a troubled home is a home in which the mother is the dominate influence. Female domination of the home is not God's method of parenting. The woman who chooses to dominate her home, in that she is the primary authority in the home, will find that her children will suffer from emotional and psychological fragmentation that will affect their over all holistic development into a healthy adult.

The second troubling side of troubled homes is the absent father. Far too many African American fathers choose not to father their children. The absence of the father creates the kind of vacuum that cannot be filled by even the best surrogate father. It is necessary for children to have both parents involved in their lives in a positive way if they are going to develop a foundation upon which a whole adult can be built.

Men who fight with their wives and beat their children are also troubling influences in the parenting process. Mothers who have multiple lovers are troubling to the parenting process also. The primary causes behind the destructive behavior of our teens are found in the nest from which these children have come.

BEYOND THE NEST

The second part of phase three in the parenting process covers ages five through twelve. In this eight-year period, the child ventures outside of the nest into kindergarten and then public school.

Parents should not expect the school system to develop the character of their children. Nor is it the responsibility of the school to give identity, values, and morals to children. Public education is to contribute to the development of the intellect, and the physical, social, and economic skills of children but it is the parent's role to shape the character of their children, by giving them value, bending their will and molding their attitude.

The education of children must involve the parents at every level. This is especially true of the African American child and most specifically the male child. For the most part, the education of black children is seriously deficient today primarily because neither the parents nor the school system are willing to invest the time and interest necessary to educate children.

It is important to emphasize again the point that schools are designed to build on the foundation that the parents have established within the child. To put it another way, it is the responsibility of teachers to cultivate the seeds of integrity, self-esteem, and values that have already been planted in the fertile soil of the child's mind. In education the teacher is a partner with the parents and God in fashioning an adult from a child who is holistically functional.

While the national discussion rages on across America regarding the quality of education available to children, a growing number of African Americans are looking to the suburban schools as an educational panacea for their children. Still other black Christians have turned to white academies as the better alternative for educating their children. The fact is for the African American parents, educating their children poses a serious challenge. For while the suburban schools may have better facilities and teachers with better credentials, the racial prejudice can be a serious deterrent to the education of black children. The white Christian academies are, for the most part, good educational institutions but again the prevalence of racism is most destructive to black children. The inner-city schools have simply been abandoned by most school boards and often, nothing good educationally really happens in those schools.

Having had children in a predominantly black school district, a white Christian academy, and a suburban public school, combined with thirty years of pastoring parents and children who attended all of the above, I am satisfied in my own mind that for African Americans the education of their children is a real challenge.

For the African American parent, navigating the challenge faced in educating their children means constantly working the home environment so that children are motivated to prioritize their education. It means reinforcing their self-esteem and filling in the historical and relational needs of the child. Both parents must involve themselves in the educational process. This involvement includes screening the assigned books that the child has to read. It means constantly monitoring the attitude of the teachers and administrators towards your child. It means being willing to confront the school board regarding the teachers and the programs being offered and see that they are fair to every student regardless of their race.

African American parents cannot afford to assume that the teachers have the best interest of their child at heart. This is seldom the case no matter the race of the teacher. It is the responsibility of the parent to see to it that the teacher delivers a quality education in a positive attitude to their child.

At the risk of being controversial, I suggest that in many instances the African American parent must take an adversarial, confrontational approach to the teachers and school administrators involved in the education of their children, with their sons in particular. The reason such an approach is often necessary is because the teachers and administrators can have both low and negative expectations of black children, and black boys in particular. The child is perceived as being intellectually deficient and physically sufficient. The parents of black children must not assume that the teachers and administrators are right when it comes to an issue involving their child.

A number of African American parents have a view of school and teachers that is reflective of a past era when teachers really cared about the child. Thus they tend to blame the child for how things go in school and take the teacher's side regarding most issues. However, in my view these are not days in which parents can afford to respond in such ways. In every issue the child must be given primary believability, for, after all, this is your child; thus you should be able to predict their attitude and behavior. I say believe the child until all of the facts say otherwise.

During this time the parent must concern themselves with the issue of discipline outside of the home. This means teaching children how to manage their attitude and behavior in the community including, but not limited to school and church. The issue of discipline has been in force since day one of the child's life; however, it is at this point that the cords of discipline are to be tightened.

Discipline includes such things as instruction, standards, restraints, and control. This form of discipline has to do with the internal control of the child that restrains the external behavior of the child while at the same time stimulating and motivating the child to strive towards that which is good.

Discipline has to do with bending the will of the child. The will of a child should not be broken but bent towards that which is good. This includes such things as respect for authority, compassion and sensitivity towards others, obedience to parents, and positive constructive attitude and behavior in their social relationships.

The goal in discipline is balance so that the child is not abused or neglected by either parent. Many times there are two extremes in the discipline of black children. The father often is an extreme disciplinarian, especially with his son, and the mother is often extremely liberal with the son in terms of discipline. This most often creates conflict in the home between father and son and mother and father regarding the son. Sometimes the spirit of the son can be broken by the father.

Parents should never punish their children but rather, they should discipline them. Punishment has in view the application of pain that is constant with the offense. Discipline, on the other hand, has in view the application of that which is unpleasant for the express purpose of effecting change in the child. When the correction is made the discipline is removed.

PARENTING IN THE CONTEXT OF A SPIRITUAL DEFICIT

The need for discipline in parenting means that the parents must have specific goals and objectives set for the children. The household must have moral, social, and ethical standards by which it operates. The expectations and limitations that are placed upon the child must be clear and so must be the consequences of not living up to these expectations.

In discipline there must be a place for what I call "wobble room" for the child. This means making allowances for the child to fail sometimes and at other times make mistakes. There are no perfect children.

Between the ages of five and twelve the parent does well to begin the process of exposing the child to a broader range of culture which includes the culture of other people. When parents travel it is a good idea to make every effort to take the child with them.

During this time children should be seriously indoctrinated in the Christian faith so that they are not only saved, but spiritually and biblically literate in the things of God. This means teaching the child the Bible and modeling what you teach them in the home and in the community.

In search of a good education for their child, a number of African American parents enroll their children in religious schools and academies that are not in agreement with their faith. This includes even some nonChristian schools. This is unwise. Children need to be seriously indoctrinated in the Christian faith and the indoctrination must be consistent.

The parent who is serious about the Christian indoctrination of their children will be very careful in their choice of the environment and sources from which their children learn about God, at least in terms of who God is and how to have a saving relationship with him that is genuine.

Here I must refer again to the spiritual deficit that characterizes the social, religious, and family context in which today's African American Christian must parent. It is wise of parents today to be sensitive to the content of the faith embraced by their own parents and siblings. It should not be assumed that what parents, sisters and brothers believe and live as it pertain to their Christian faith is fit for your children. Often it happens that what grandparents do and say combined with what aunts and uncles do and say creates serious conflicts in the mind of children who are genuinely born-again.

Many African Americans will argue with some validity that parenting is a communal or village responsibility. In North American today the village idea of yesterday contains a multitude of flaws and dangers.

Christian indoctrination of children requires a household in which the father is a committed Christian. The family must all be in the same church and believe the same thing about Christ, salvation, the Bible and how to live in fellowship with God.

In all too many instances the extended family of born-again believers poses a serious threat to the indoctrination of their children. This threat is evident in the liberal doctrine, lifestyle, and attitude towards things that are spiritual. It is also evident in the passive female-dominated brand of Christianity that is embraced by a number of church members.

This is not to suggest that the born-again believer act in ways that are offensive to their family. Nor does it imply that the African American Christian does their parenting in a vacuum. It is simply to suggest that in the context of today's religious ideology the African American Christian must make every effort to seriously and thoroughly indoctrinate their children.

There is much concern in the Christian community about the impact of the million man march, under the leadership of the Nation of Islam, on the minds of young African American men. The million man march was a good thing in many ways. However, it is what the Muslim faith teaches and believes about deity of Jesus the Christ that is damning for all who embrace that faith. It is the indoctrination of our children that is the strongest defense the Christian faith has against the continued influence of the Islamic faith among young black men.

I have found over and over again that it is when the young black men and women go off to college that they are seriously confronted for the first time about the validity of their Christian faith. Sadly, in all too many instances the young college freshman is ill-equipped to defend his or her faith.

CHAPTER 22

MANAGING THE DEVELOPMENT PROCESS

This six-year period covers the years of puberty and the initial move into full adulthood. It is during this time that parents begin to see the evidence of what they have been doing with their children. In this fourth phase of parenting the child is evidencing the coming together of the combined evolution of *nature* and *nurture* that have been brought together in the child in the home environment. The most significant aspect of this evolution is the home environment in which the child is growing up.

These years are the management years because it is the time in which not as much is taught and learned in this phase. This is a period in which the parent is confronted with the character, attitude, values, behavior, and belief system that the child has been given in the home environment. At best the parent will succeed at managing all of this so that the child moves on into adulthood. However it is here that a number of parents recognize that they have lost their child to the world.

During this phase of development a number of children explode into full-blown rebellion against all authority and reject even their parents, choosing instead to move out into the streets rather than live under the authority of the parents. Managing rebellion in children is a difficult challenge for parents, and yet it must be done.

I watched William and his little sister Jill grow from

the time they were babies. They were ideal children from all appearances. When William turned thirteen he changed from a mild-mannered, obedient boy to a stubborn and disobedient out-of-control tyrant.

William and his sister had grown up in a home that was dysfunctional. It was an environment of hostility, strict and unreasonable demands, and an environment in which forgiveness was not a reality. Around the age of thirteen something new showed up inside of William and shortly thereafter that same thing showed up in his sister Jill. This new thing was the arrival of puberty in which the hormones of these children begin to make themselves present and active.

It is not possible to describe the trauma that the parents of these two children experienced as they watched their children openly reject all that they had publicly stood for as committed church people. In reality these parents had planted in their children the seeds of rebellion and bitterness in the early years of their lives. When puberty arrived the parents could not manage neither the rage from within caused by the dysfunctional environment in which the children were nurtured or the rage caused by the arrival of puberty.

Here it is important to mention something to single mothers and mothers who tend to dominate their husbands. In most instances the dysfunctional environment alone is sufficient to create an uncontrollable child by the early teen years. However, when it happens that a boy enters puberty, not only does his voice change but he most often becomes beyond the management skills of his mother. In other words, most single mothers tend to lose control of their sons when they reach the teen years.

I can well remember the day when the phone rang and on the other end was Bob screaming at the top of his lungs, "I will kill him! I will kill him!" "What is the matter with you, Bob?" I yelled back into the phone. "This boy of mine has tried to fight me! I will kill him!" again Bob screamed into the phone. "You had better get over here quick before I kill this little nigger!"

When I arrived at Bob's house and finally got him to settle down I listened to an all too familiar story. Bob had a history of fighting his wife and threatening his children. On this day when he went into his rage of anger his son

PARENTING IN THE CONTEXT OF A SPIRITUAL DEFICIT

stood up to him and dared him to hit his mother again. The boy then told his dad in no uncertain terms that he was not going to do anything to either him, his sister, or his mother anymore. From that day on Bob and his son lived in the same house but as hostile enemies of each other. Bob had raised a son that he could not manage. In fact, the son began to manage Bob in his fits of rage.

At this stage of parenting, effective parenting means effective management of the children in view of what has been planted in the child and the natural emergence of hormonal changes in the child. This is a full-time responsibility for both parents.

The first thing that must be managed is the child's attitude. The attitude is a picture of the disposition of the child. How children have been shaped in their character will show up in this phase of life. This is the stage where how children feels about themselves begins to show. The attitudes toward the opposite sex begins to shift. The values that have been transmitted begin to show in the choice of friends and habits. This is also the stage in which the child begins to think more about their own sexuality.

When Mark's son reached this age his mother was outraged at the fact that she had observed their son a few times looking and touching his genitals. In addition the boy began to show a strong interest in girls and express a desire to spend time outside of the home with other boys. Well, his mother was having none of that so she demanded that Mark have a talk with their son and lay down the law that such behavior would not be tolerated.

What Mark's wife wanted was for their son to remain on the other side of puberty. This was not to be. I suggested to Mark that he insist that his wife let the boy alone and allow him to grow up. In addition I said that he and his wife had been good parents to their children. I was confident that puberty would not wipe out what they had instilled in your children.

During this phase it is imperative that the parent be involved with the child. Parents must strive to have a level of involvement with the child that allows the child the freedom and the opportunity to see, ask questions, and learn how to manage themselves according to their gender. This means that both the daughters and the sons are involved with their mother and their father.

At this stage of life the greatest threat to black boys is the absent and/or uninvolved father. This absence or uninvolvement by the African American father will most often allow the son to be managed by a somebody who does not understand the boy. In all too many cases that somebody is the athletic coach at the school who, in many instances, is white and more committed to his own career than he is to any of his students.

In terms of effective parenting, from public school to college the African American male child has far too many coaches filling the role of father in involvement in their lives. This open door is created by the uninvolvement of the African American father in the lives of their sons.

The argument can be made that athletics have been for a number of African American boys and girls their ticket out of poverty. However it is evident that for a number of these successful athletes their white coaches and managers have been the greater beneficiaries. There is very little evidence that the long-standing tremendous success of blacks in athletics has benefited the African- American community in any significant way. These professional athletes tend to follow the counsel of their couches and managers and invest where they tell them to.

As a father I have made every effort to discourage my son from becoming seriously involved in sports. I also sought to diminish the influence of coaches in the life of my son. I would feel cheated if my son was closer to his athletic coach than he was to me because of the involvement of the couch in his life. The involvement of the parent with the child is as important to the daughter as it is with the son. Daughters need their father to love them and give them a sense of significance, a sense of belonging, and a sense of security. Fathers who do not provide this for their daughters will most often find their daughters looking to some other man for these things.

Parents must manage the behavior of their children during this stage of their development. This means communicating to the child in a positive way a respect for authority, a principle that has been established in phases one and two. Parents need to communicate the limitations and expectations that the child will be held to. The flipside of this management is communicating the consequences that will result from misbehaving privately or publicly.

PARENTING IN THE CONTEXT OF A SPIRITUAL DEFICIT

The goal of the parent is to manage the external expression of the internal evaluation and changes that are occurring in the child. This means being willing and able to hold the children accountable for their behavior. Here it is necessary that parents take the necessary steps to be available to monitor the behavior of their children.

It happened one day that the school called to inquire about the absence of one of our children from school. Betty and I were more than a little bit surprised to hear that our child was not at school since Betty had dropped them all off that morning. That evening after school our children came out and stood in the usual place to be picked up by their mother. However, this day, much to their surprise, it was their father and not their mother who was there to pick them up.

When I inquired about how school went that day the child responded in the usual way—"Fine." After a while I said that I had been informed that my child had skipped school that day. In our home, the consequences for lying about being in school were much more severe than was the act of skipping school. Skipping school was out of bounds but lying was a technical foul that carried serious consequences. Needless to say the response from both Betty and I to this situation insured that, to our knowledge at least, it was never repeated. Management of childhood behavior means being available to get involved any time and any place when a child's behavior is involved.

When my son was in junior high school, the school nurse called and said to me, "Mr. Lane, your son has been in a fight and he needs to go to the hospital. He has a cut behind his ear." I said to the teacher, "I will be in your office within twenty minutes."

When I arrived at the school I immediately asked my son what happened. He told me that a couple of boys had jumped him in the rest room and that the teachers, after observing that the perpetrators were all black, turned their heads and left them to fight it out. Having heard that, I went straight to the principal's office and demanded to see him personally. After much waiting, I finally got my meeting with the principal.

I informed the principal of what my son had told me and I noted in particular that I believed my son and would believe him unless I had solid evidence to the contrary.

And there was no evidence to the contrary. I left the principal's office and went to the school administration building and presented my case to the superintendent. I made sure the superintendent understood that should this kind of thing ever happened again I would seek damages against everyone involved.

The point of this story is to emphasize the fact that fathers must involve themselves in the affairs of their sons and, in so doing, the fathers must know that their sons place a high value on truth and honesty. In this situation I knew full well that my son would fight if he was provoked. I also knew that he was not given to lying.

It is important that parents know their children to the point that they can predict in most cases what the child will and will not do. Thus in terms of behavior, parents need to have in their minds a category of not likely, improbable, maybe, possible and probable. It is important to children that their parents believe and trust them.

CHAPTER 23

MANAGING THE EDUCATION OF THE CHILD

The education of African American children is a major challenge for parents for a number of reasons. The general powerlessness of African American people is a major hindrance to the education of black children. America's social, economic, educational, and political polity, as well as white supremacy, all play a role in maintaining the powerlessness of black people in America.

It is no secret that approximately forty to sixty percent of all state and federal prisoners are young African American boys and men. In addition, a third or more of all African American men are in some way tied to the justice system as a parolee or former inmate. Black on black crime, absentee fathers, and unwed mothers are all reflections of a powerless people who are victims of that state of powerlessness. Thus in terms of education, the African American parent faces a strong challenge.

Growing up in the forties and fifties my education took place in a segregated context. There was no semblance of equality between the facilities, teachers, and general environment between the white and black school system. In twelve years of public education I cannot remember even once receiving a new textbook. In East Carol Parish in northern Louisiana, all the textbooks were first sent to the white school system and then in a few years when they got new books, we got their old out-dated ones.

In those days when the teachers often had only an eight grade education and my father was functionally illiterate and could not even write his name, I received a basic educational foundation upon which all of my life experiences have been built. The quality of my educational foundation was not found in the inferior schools that I attended as a child. My educational foundation is rooted in the environment my parents created—they loved and empowered me to strive for the best in life, maximizing whatever resources were available to me.

Most of the local and national African American leaders today are from the south and were educated in is public school systems not unlike mine. Todays African American parents do not have to contend with separate and unequal public school systems for their children as I did, and there are few external legal restrictions and limitations on black children today compared to when I grew up. Yet the African American parent is producing few children who are literate. The question is why?

In answering, one must acknowledge the reality of racism and its continued negative impact on the availability of equal education for African American children. However, the more serious hindrance to the education of black children is the failure of the parents to take an active role in the education of the children. The value that parents place on education is passed on to the children.

This is the phase of parenting where the parents are managing the education of the child by means of involvement in the educational process. This includes such things as choosing the courses the child takes each semester, guiding the child's involvement in sports and other activities, supervising the child's choice of books to read and monitoring the teachers professionalism with the child .

The parent must develop expectations of the child that are consistent with the child's ability to perform academically. The parents must insist that the teacher's expectations of the child are consistent with the child's ability and are not regulated by race or social class.

MANAGING THE CHOICE OF FRIENDS

Most parents know that when their children are small they need consistent care and supervision. In providing this, parents carefully choose those people with whom they will entrust their children. This care for small children is considered to be the substance of good parenting.

As children grow older parents tend to become less and less concerned about their care and supervision as it pertains to who the child spends time with. The general consensus is that as children grow older they are increasingly able to care for themselves in their dealings with other people.

This kind of thinking is flawed. This fourth phase of parenting that encompasses ages 13 to 19 requires as much care and supervision as did phase one. For while in phase one the concern is about what others may do to the young child, the concern in this phase is about what the child may do to him or herself.

First Corinthians 15:33 says, "Do not be deceived, bad company corrupts good morals." This passage refers to the corrupting influence of false doctrine that denies the resurrection of Jesus from the dead. The point of the passage is that Christians who choose to be friends with those who deny the reality of the resurrection of Jesus Christ would ultimately be drawn into that heresy. Those who denied the resurrection were classified in the Christian community as bad company.

In the African American community there are those young people who, because of their attitude and behavior, must be classified as bad company. Such young people would include those who are not saved, those who are immoral, drug and alcohol users, and those who have no goals in life that point towards success. It is important to note here that the focus is not on either race or social class, but rather on the character and conduct of the child.

The principle here is simply this: *The company your children choose to keep will ultimately affect their belief system.* In most instances this means that the child will begin to question and hold suspect the principles that the parents have taught. This means that their son or daughter who has friends who do drugs is more likely to try drugs. The same is true with sex, alcohol, and affiliation with gangs.

The involvement of the parents is a strong asset in a child's choice of friends. Parents must act on the fact that they have been the same age as their children are in this phase but their children have never been their age. Drawing upon their past experience and their current sense of the times in which they live can enable the parent to share in their child's choice of friends.

Proverbs 28:7 says, "He who keeps the law is a discerning son, but he who is a companion of gluttons humiliates his father." In this proverb the distinction is drawn between a son who elects to live life by the biblical principles that his father taught him and a son who rejects the teaching of his father, choosing instead to develop friendship with unprincipled people. This second son will become an embarrassment to his father.

The principle is clear—namely that the friends chosen by children have tremendous influence on the belief system, attitude, and behavior of the child. Thus it is imperative that parents be active participants in their children's choice of friends.

Clarence was the oldest child of his middle class parents. His father was a very proud black man who not only had his clothes tailor-made, he also had Clarence's suits tailor-made. When Clarence reached his mid-teens he decided, with the permission of his parents, to get a job working on the river. The men who worked on the river were not known for their moral behavior. They were rough and tough men. They cursed, drank, and practiced immorality until they ran out of money.

By the time Clarence reached his twenties, to the surprise and dismay of his proud middle-class family, he had become in attitude and behavior what these men were. His father's disappointment turned into bitterness and they hardly spoke to each other even though they lived in the same house. It was evident to his father that this son did not share his values.

MANAGING THE ARRIVAL OF HORMONES AND DATING

In this section it is necessary to begin with a technical explanation of the hormones that have to do with sex and also to expand my discussion of the arrival and impact of puberty. The sex hormones begin to evidence their presence in the biological development of the child during puberty. Puberty usually begins during this fourth phase of the childhood development process.

Sex hormones, which are essential for the normal development and function of the reproductive system, are produced mainly by the male and female sex organs, otherwise known as gonads. Biochemically, these hormones are steroids; they are known as androgens, estrogens, and progesterone. The hypothalamus and pituitary regulate the secretion of these sex hormones at puberty and during the reproductive phase of adulthood. Also, the adrenal cortex of both sexes produces small quantities of androgens and progesterone.

Parents must understand and accept the fact that their child will, in the natural flow of development, begin to evidence an interest in sex and sexuality. The most common expression of this interest can be seen in the child's growing interest in the opposite sex. For most children the secretion of sex hormones begins at puberty. It cannot be delayed by the parent and it cannot be hurried by the child. This development is a normal part of the overall growth process of the child.

It is the arrival of puberty and the accompanying explosion of sex hormones in the child that necessitates aggressive management of the child's social life by the parent. Parents must know and respond to the reality that at this early age, their child not only has an interest in sex and sexuality but they also have the ability to impregnate or become pregnant.

In the normal flow of things, girls develop faster than boys. During this phase of development the girl will likely be much more developed physically in terms of breast, hips and overall physical development. She will be taller than the boys her age and evidence an interest in boys that is not consistent with the interest of the boys her age towards her. The faster development of girls than boys can often cause a girl to develop a relationship with a boy who is older than she. These kind of relationships are very risky to the girl in terms of her ability to manage herself in a social situation.

Likewise, it is not unusual to find boys at this age developing relationships with girls who are younger than they are. Younger girls are likely to be more tolerant of the naiveté of the young man than would a girl his own age.

This physiological development of boys and girls at this age places an increased demand on the parents in terms of their availability to manage the child. Parents must be mindful of the fact that at this age they still have children, and not miniature adults. The highest risk the child faces at this age is from within the child's own development. This development will take place no matter how prepared or unprepared the parents are to manage it.

Parent must carefully define and establish the boundaries and limitations the child must abide by. For example, children should only have the option to date. Courtship is an option limited for adults who are empowered with the ability to choose a mate and establish their own family.

Dating is best viewed as a social term that has to do primarily with entertaining and being entertained. It is getting together for the purpose of socializing. It involves attitudes, values, moral, and spiritual convictions. Healthy dating is best done with friends, and never strangers.

Going steady must be distinguished from dating. It is best understood to mean courtship. Courtship is a specific choice of and attachment to a particular individual with whom there has come to be a binding, two-way commitment. Courtship by it's very nature must have as it's ultimate goal marriage. This is not a relationship for children who are in puberty. Children who opt to go steady will most often apply the rules and standards of courtship to their relationship.

It is wise for parents to manage their children during this stage of their development with very strict lines of accountability and responsibility. The consequences of disregarding established expectations and limitations must be consistently applied.

Managing the child's life in this stage means asking questions about the child's choice of friends, places of socialization, and the kind of entertainment the child's friends like.

By the time Yvette reached age fourteen she was fully developed physically, so much so that she looked like a young woman. As a very beautiful black girl, Yvette attracted no small amount of attention from young men, most of whom were much older than she was.

Yvette's parents were both professional people seriously involved in their professions. Neither had the time to invest in managing the life of this beautiful young girl. By her eighteenth birthday Yvette had given birth to two children.

In the minds of her parents, their daughter had low morals. However, it was not Yvette's morals that were the problem. The real problem was the poorly managed hormones that were present in Yvette's stage of development. This young girl did not spoil her life because she was less moral than other girls. Her future was stifled by the parental undermanagement of this phase of her life.

Few boys were more handsome as Billy. He got a job at one of the local grocery stores and worked as a stock clerk. In the store his tall statue, and well-built body caused him to stand out even in a crowd.

In short order Bill's handsome appearance got the consistent attention of the women who frequented the store. Many of the women who flirted with Billy had children who were as old and even older than he. In time, Billy's exploding hormones combined with the poor management of his life by his mother got him in moral trouble.

Parents must make every effort to work with their children, even when the child rejects their involvement to manage their social life during puberty. The idea that it is unreasonable to expect children not to have sex during this phase of life is mere stupidity. This is a stage of development in which the child's passion for sex rides on the wings of curiosity. Abstinence is the only option. Anything else is close to sexual abuse and exploitation.

Managing Peer Pressure

In the context of relationships a peer is one with whom there is a shared equality in terms of vocation, life-style, and social class. It is a group of people with whom one feels and experiences a sense of belonging, security, and significance. Inherent in the very idea of peers is the psychological pressure to acquire and maintain equality with the members of the group and thereby achieve this sense of belonging, security, and significance.

There is in children a kind of cruelty towards each other that causes them to demand conformity to the group or else experience rejection by that group. At this age few children are emotionally equipped to deal with rejection, thus conformity is the normal response.

Empowering the child to manage peer pressure means having developed the kind of relationship with the child that causes the child to feel that they belong, they are secure, and they are significant at home. The goal is to help the child manage peer pressure. It is not possible to prevent it.

Joe and Tracy had two children—a girl and a boy. They were very protective parents with their children. Tracy decided what both children would wear and who they would play with. This worked fine until their son reached the age of puberty. As a teenage African American boy, the styles and attitudes of his peers began to evidence itself in his choice of dress, hairstyle, walk, and vocabulary. This change in their son was very unsettling.

In my consultation with this couple I suggested to them that their son's conformity to the pressure of his peers might suggest a deficit in their relationship with their children. Joe and Tracy were good parents but they had not taken the time to develop the kind of relationship with their son that made him feel that he belonged, and that he was secure and significant. Joe was the kind of father who worked all the time. His idea of being a good father was ninety-nine percent provider and one percent involvement with his son.

In terms of managing peer pressure the role of the parent is one of supportive involvement with the child at the emotional, intellectual, and companionship levels. In most instances in homes where hearts are more important than heads, the child will tend to conform less to their peer group when the demands of the group are in conflict with the expectations of the parents at home.

In addition to peer pressure, the parent must assist the child in managing the pressure of developing and maintaining relationships and the pressure of academic and social skills. In all of these areas the parent must be a supportive participant with the child.

My wife and I were surprised to discover that when our children did not have a date or did not receive phone calls from significant people in their world they felt rejected and depressed. In college our children were often left out of a gathering of black students because they would not participate in what the group did. The thing that made the difference in how they turned out was the nature of our relationship with them.

NURTURING SPIRITUAL DEVELOPMENT

It is not unusual for children to lose some of their enthusiasm for church during this phase of their development. This decline in interest should not alarm the parents. It can be difficult for children to maintain a strong spiritual focus when everything inside of them is exploding and they have a declining sense of who they are. This is a time when the child is between a full-fledged child and a full-grown adult. It is an age that is tremendously confusing and frustrating to the child. Thus parents should not be alarmed when they discover that spiritual things have moved to the back of their children's mind.

For the African American parent the role of the father must become that of being the primary nurturer of the spiritual development of the children. No amount of church-going by the mother can substitute for the genuine spiritual leadership of the father in the development of the children.

The African American parent must be ever-mindful of the fact that in the black church the women outnumber the men almost eight to one—that is, eight black women to every one black man in the church. This absence of male membership in the black church is passed from father to son, one generation after another. Perhaps it is this lack of spiritual involvement combined with a lack of biblically-based convictions that contributes significantly to the social, domestic, economic, and moral dilemma in our community.

While the black church has a membership where women outnumber men on average, the Nation of Islam has a membership in which men out number women on average eight to one. The fact that black men are increasingly attracted to the Nation of Islam might well suggest that future generations of black families will be increasingly Muslim. The prospect of this possibility eventually will be deterred only by the Christian disciplining of children by their parents.

GUARDING THE HEART OF THE CHILD

Proverbs 4:23 exhorts us to "Watch over your heart with all diligence, for from it flow the springs of life." The idea here is that the heart is the center of a person's thought processes. It is the seat of integrity, for in the heart decisions are made with regard to right and wrong.

Mark 7:21-23 says, "For from within, out of the heart of men, proceed the evil thoughts, fornications, thefts, murders, adulteries, deeds of coveting and wickedness, as well as deceit, sensuality, envy, slander, pride and foolishness. All these evil things proceed from within and defile the man." This passage is saying that the truest expression of a person's character is what is in their heart. It is also saying that what is in the heart is expressed in word, attitude, and deed.

During this fourth phase of parenting the parent must strive with all diligence to guard the heart of the child against the influence of evil. This is a period in which the child is very gullible and is easily impressed and influenced with either good or evil. This is a time when the father must make every effort to be involved with his children, both guarding and protecting their heart. The heart of the daughter must be guarded against the power and influence of infatuation. During this period girls need to feel loved and accepted. They need a lot of hugging and reassuring. They need to feel secure and wanted. These felt needs in girls most often puts their hearts at risk. To minimize this risk fathers do well to love their daughters and express that love by being involved in their world.

This need for parental love and support is also true of boys during this period. Thus mothers do well to lead in the expression of love for the son. This love is best expressed by whole-hearted involvement in his world.

As a father I contended for the hearts of my children. I wanted to be their hero, their source of strength and security. I did not want my daughters to ever feel the kind of vacuum in their lives that caused them to pursue a relationship with a man just to feel secure and significant. I did not want my son to feel that he could not talk to me about anything at any time. I sought to be the kind of father that could not be replaced by an athletic coach at school. I wanted to be my son's model of manhood.

In striving to be all that a father should be to his children, I made it a habit to adjust my schedule so that I could give attention to such things as choice of friends, dating, and phone calls, and I made a practice of taking my children with me to conventions and on vacations.

To guard the heart of the child the parent must be always be the adult and the parent in the relationship. The parent must be a good listener to the child and very observant of the ways of the child. The parent must be sensitive to the child's moods and be involved with them in the development of their social skills.

When Millicent arrived at college she found the lobby crawling with "lobby lizards." "Lobby lizards" describes the men who hang out on college campuses seeking to exploit the freshman class. These young men seem to have an acquired ability in sorting out and making contact with those girls whose hearts are not being guarded well.

Millicent was such a young woman. Her heart was exposed, and in short order she was being exploited by a few of these young men. In addition to getting pregnant and having twins, Millicent dropped out of college and became a teenage wife and mother. The trouble was, when Millicent lost her heart, she also lost control of the source of her life. It is difficult to build a positive life with a broken and bitter heart.

Mike thought he could handle life because he was a man and in his family men were taught how to be "real men." By the time Mike reached age eighteen he had fathered several children and was no longer sure about his future. Parents must understand that the heart of boys must be guarded just as strictly as girls. A young man with a broken heart is just as likely to lose his spirit and motivation to succeed as are girls.

CHAPTER 24

THE COMPLETED PRODUCT

The goal of parenting is to develop a whole adult person who is not fragmented and who is fully equipped to function in the social, economical, domestic, political, and cultural environment in which they must live. This process begins early on in the child's life and continues through age twenty-two.

The idea in effective parenting is not for parents to reproduce duplicates of themselves—such an effort is most often futile. The goal is to develop a whole person uniquely fitted to their own personality and yet in possession of the legacy passed down from their ancestors.

During their late teen years the child has been in transition from childhood to adulthood. At this point the parent must recognize that they are no longer dealing with a child but a young adult. While it is true that the young adult will evolve more fully into adulthood in the next few years, this is nonetheless an adult.

At the very least the completed product should have a profile that indicates that this young adult person is one who places a high value on their relationship with God. This priority on the spiritual not only includes the value that they place on their relationship with God but also on His Word in maintaining a positive testimony before the world. This young adult should be one who places high value on their parents, At the very least this is a basic biblical profile of a whole and healthy young adult.

PARENTING IN THE CONTEXT OF A SPIRITUAL DEFICIT

According to Proverbs 4:20-22, the child that learns wisdom and keeps that wisdom at the very center of their heart will experience physical, emotional, and spiritual wholeness.

A number of parents never really finish parenting. This is especially true of mothers. However, even though parents will always be parents, they will not always be in the process of parenting. This process ends when the child reaches chronological adulthood.

THE TRANSFER OF AUTHORITY TO THE CHILD

This final phase of parenting covers ages nineteen to twenty-two. At this point the parent needs to move forward in the process of treating the son or daughter as an adult. This means giving up the reins of parental authority and handing them over to the son or daughter. It is time to allow the child to practice their own convictions, values and lifestyle, without parental supervision.

During this phase of parenting it is absolutely necessary for parents to realize that they are moving from having the role of authority over the child to being in a partnership with the child. At this stage the parent's ideas and convictions become increasingly suggestions to the child, not orders or commands. The choice and the final decision in the matter belongs to the son or daughter and not the parents.

This is a difficult time for parents for, in those cases where there are children of different ages in the home, the parent must practice different stages of parenting. It is not wise to continue parenting all the siblings in the same way when they are in different phases of development.

Wilena was a good mother to her children in every way, however, it was difficult to tell her that her twenty year old daughter no longer needed her to make the decisions about her life. Wilena's problem was that she had no life apart from her children; thus they were doomed to being forever under her authority. This is not wise.

Parents should understand effective parenting to mean developing children who as adults will be equipped to function independent of the authority of their parents. Children should always respect their parents but they must have the freedom to be their own people.

The Completed Product

When our youngest daughter was twenty-two she decided that she wanted to get married. She brought home the young man whom she had chosen to become her husband. At the time my daughter was away in college and I had met this young man just once. I knew nothing about him. As is the custom in our house, when decisions of such magnitude are being considered, we gather as a family to discuss the matter. My oldest daughter and her husband, my son, and my wife and I all gathered with my youngest daughter and her man of choice to hear their story.

When all was said and done I said to my daughter, "I do not know this young man and I cannot therefore give my consent." With this said, my daughter angrily burst into tears. I was aware of the fact that the ultimate decision was my daughter's to make, yet I was confident that her respect for me as her father would not allow her to proceed with her marriage plans. The point is while parents must not dominate the decisions of their adult children, most children will respect the wisdom of their parents in major things if the parents do not attempt to control everything.

This principle of transferring authority to a child came up in our family when our son decided that he wanted to have his ear pierced. In addition he wanted to change his wardrobe to a more contemporary look. In my view this was a matter that involved his body and, at his age, these things were his choice.

Assisting in the Choice of College

The idea of college for a number of parents is given far less consideration than it is due. This is especially true as it pertains to the African American male. There should be no question that the child will attend school and graduate. There should be no question that the young man/woman will attend college or trade school. The commitment of both the parent and the son or daughter to finishing college or trade school should be just as solid as the commitment to finish high school

The choice of college is important for a number of reason, not the least of which is the quality of product the college produces in terms of employability. Some colleges and trade schools do not produce graduates who are likely to find employment in their field of training.

It is equally important that parents assist their children in choosing a college that is balanced in its cross cultural mix. One-race colleges are often quite limited in their ability to equip students to participate in a world economy. However, on campuses where the student is a minority, there is a strong likelihood that those fields that offer a more lucrative financial future could be institutionally off-limits for the black student.

It was the desire of my oldest daughter to be an occupational therapist from her early childhood. During high school she won a number of awards in the field of medical care. She attended a predominantly African American high school with all African American faculty.

Her vocational choice took her to a predominantly white university. My daughter was hardly prepared emotionally for the trauma she was to experience there. Once she made known her vocational choice, the department determined that neither she nor the other sixty-five or so black students who chose to major in Occupational Therapy, would succeed. Because of this, she was advised to take difficult courses that she would not otherwise have needed to take. She was counseled to give up trying to become a therapist and become instead an assistant.

Fortunately for my daughter she had a father who was able to pay for her college education without any grants or loans. Those black students who needed grants and loans were forced out of the program because they could not earn the grade point average necessary to maintain the loans and grants. The result was that my daughter was one of only two or three African Americans to finish the occupational therapy program at this university.

Few African American parents are aware of the pressures and subtle racist behavior that their children face in predominantly white colleges and universities. Such knowledge is essential for parents to have so they can equip their children to succeed.

ASSISTING IN PAYING TUITION

The cost of a college education is far more than any student can afford on their own. Parents must share in paying the cost of and education. Paying college tuition is inherent in the parenting process.

It is not unusual to find parents willing to pay the tuition for their daughters but the son's tuition tends to be another matter. The African American parent must determine that the college education of their son is equally important to that of the daughter.

In paying the tuition, the parent allows the student time to give more attention to their studies. This should allow them to pursue vocations that require more difficult studies.

STOP THE PARENTING: BECOME A SUPPORTIVE COUNSELOR

The parent who does not intend to parent all of their children's lives must grow their children into whole, functional adults. Thus parents must have a goal to equip their children with the necessary survival skills that empowers them to leave home and make it on their own.

Parents who do not plan to spend all of their life parenting must have life goals that extend beyond the years of growing children into adults. Parents should stop parenting their own children when they reach adulthood. This means, by the way, that they should definitely not raise their grandchildren.

It is the view of a number of African American parents that they are always responsible for their children in terms of providing, protecting, and nurturing. I am not of that opinion. The role of parents in the lives of their adult children is one of a supportive counselor. It is not possible to develop adult children who are already fully developed. It is possible to support children as the branch out on their own.

As difficult as it may be for some parents, they must stay out of the affairs of their children as an authority. Their involvement in the affairs of their children must be as an invited counselor.

ESTABLISH AN ADULT RELATIONSHIP

It is imperative that parents realize that parenting is an important aspect of marriage. However, it is at best a secondary marriage responsibility. The primary focus and responsibility of marriage is the couple themselves.

Developing and maintaining a strong healthy marriage relationship must always be the primary focus of the couple. In the home the strongest love relationship must be and remain between the man and his wife. It must never become the mother and her children or vise versa.

When it happens as it so often does in the African-American family that the strongest love relationship is between the mother and her children that mother will feel compelled to maintain a parenting relationship with her children no matter their age.

In order to establish an adult relationship with children both parents must begin the process of disengaging their parenting efforts as the child moves into their teen years. Thus when the child leaves home, the parent is able to gradually stop their parenting in view of the evident maturity of the child.

To establish an adult relationship with the child the parent must recognize and respect the child as an adult. This means treating the child as an equal in every way. The parent must respect the child's privacy and allow the child to develop and live their own life-style. Finally the parent must free the child up so that he or she has the liberty to make their own life choices even though they may be different from their parents.

Part 6

Where Do We Go From Here?

CHAPTER 25

PARENTING IN THE 21ST CENTURY

Almost thirty years ago a book was written about the African American family entitled, *The Moynihan Report and The Politics of Controversy*. Lee Rainwater and William Yancy published this report in 1967. Daniel P. Moynihan is a democratic senator from New York state. He is also a recognized sociologist who has served in different capacities with three different presidents.

In his report (that was subsequently published in book form by Rainwater and Yancy at the height of the Civil Rights movement), Mr. Moynihan gave a bleak outlook for the future of the African American family. He spoke prophetically regarding its future and in his view the African American family was and would continue to be in what he called a tangle of pathology. This tangle of pathology was most evident in the family structure of those he referred to as the "lower class blacks." At the time of his writing he contended that the family structure of the lower class blacks in many urban centers was approaching complete breakdown.

He further noted that the black community was divided into two distinct groups; namely an emerging middle class that places a higher premium on family stability and the conserving of family resources than do white middle class families. Second, he saw an increasing disorganized and disadvantaged lower class group.

PARENTING IN THE CONTEXT OF A SPIRITUAL DEFICIT

The root causes of the failing structure of the black family as described in the Moynihan report were slavery, reconstruction, urbanization, unemployment/poverty and the unequal wage system in corporate America. Having set forth what he believed to be the root causes behind the crumbling structure of the black family, Moynihan dared to speak prophetically of the future of the black family. This was at best a "tangle of pathology" which was based on matriarchy, the failure of youth, delinquency and crime, the armed forces, and alienation.

I read this report and, like most of my associates, I reacted with critical evaluations of the report and ultimately rejected it totally as being harsh and unfair. In retrospect I am not sure that my reaction to the Moynihan report was entirely objective. It may well be that the current state of affairs in the African American family is reflective of what was predicted by the Moynihan report.

My outright rejection of the Moynihan's report has been transformed into questions as I look at the current state of affairs in the black family and then look back at the report. Since it was written and published during the height of the Civil Rights Movement, I wonder what it was that Moynihan knew that caused him to conclude that the civil rights, political, educational, and economic victories would not significantly alter the pathological state of affairs in the structure of the black family?

Perhaps Moynihan saw what Bill Moyers focused on in his more recent documentary on the black family "Black Men: An Endangered Species." In this documentary Moyer focused on the disenfranchised black men who were of the lower class described in Moynihan's earlier report. These men demonstrated a propensity for disregarding their role and responsibility as fathers to the children they fathered by women to whom they were not married. To a large degree, Moyer's documentary demonstrated from his perspective the coming to fruition of the collapse of the family structure among the lower class blacks.

Any subjective look at the African American community will evidence two distinct family groups. There is a middle class and a lower class group of people in the black community. These two groups have very different acceptable family structures and their value system is also very different. Among the lower class the family structure is in shambles. The middle class struggles, but more often manages to maintain a stable family structure.

While the size of the black middle class is debatable, it is clear that the largest group of people in the black community are not middle class. This means that the lower class represents the largest group of families in the black community. The structure of these families is seriously unstable and dysfunctional. This group is largely dependent upon government assistance due to unemployment Thus they are seriously impacted by government policies.

The 21st century must have government policies that are accessible for the lower class black families and must include jobs and assistance that empower black men to support their families. The assistance that is provided by the state and federal government must be designed to keep the man in the house and the family together. This means jobs for the parents and day care for the children.

While the government must develop more user-friendly family policies designed to empower the poor to stabilize their families, there is much to be done by middle-class blacks. The black middle class must get over it's love affair with the kind of idealism that denies the reality of poverty among a number of blacks. The middle class must realize that the family structure of many urban people is in shambles and must be attended to. While the lower class blacks may be disenfranchised and powerless in the political arena, the middle class is neither disenfranchised not powerless. Thus the middle class must use their power and influence to empower the poor blacks in the community. This empowerment will enable black men to parent the children they father.

THE EVANGELICAL CHURCH

There is little doubt in the minds of most Christians that there is a shortage of families that model the nuclear family. A nuclear family consists of a man, his wife and their children. In the African American community there is a shortage of models of this type of family structure in both the middle and lower class group. The nuclear family is nonetheless God's ideal of family structure among all people, regardless of race, class of culture.

The primary goal of the evangelical church in the 21st

century must be to increase the number of nuclear families. I believe this building process must begin in the local church with the pastor and his family. It is absolutely imperative that the pastor model the biblical ideal idea of family structure. This is not an appeal for perfection, but rather an appeal for holding the pastor to a standard of family structure and function that is just as consistent with Scripture as is his doctrine of sanctification, both in private and in public.

The evangelical church must have leaders who model the nuclear family ideal. Equipped with this group of models the local church should proceed to develop the kind of premarital and marital counseling that prepares perspective couples for a lifetime commitment to each other. It is the couple's love for each other that provides the kind of environment in which effective parenting can be accomplished. The pastor must emphasize the importance of spirituality because the three most determinative factors in the Christian home are the submissiveness of the wife, the expressed love of the father, and the obedience of the children. These three virtues are all the results of a spirit- filled life (Eph. 5:18-6:4). To the extent that the family practice the spirit-filled life, the modeling process will be enhanced.

Since the nuclear family is vanishing in the black community and, in spite of the number of family enrichment seminars that are offered, the local church must assume it's responsibility of promoting and nurturing the nuclear family with strong biblical teaching.

In the 21st century the local church must be more relevant in it's programs. The church will of necessity have to develop an outreach program that will attract people and bring them to Christ. This evangelistic outreach must go where black men are, including prisons.

The church will need to utilize its facilities on a daily basis making available to the family a holistic ministry that includes family counseling, social gatherings, family entertainment, and a host of other activities. This means that the long tradition of a strong pulpit ministry will have to be balanced with a strong family-oriented and family-focused ministry.

Fatherhood in the 21st Century

It has long been said that in the African American family the woman is the dominant force. For the most part this is a long-standing stereotype designed to reflect the powerlessness of black men. However, it is true that in the African American family the female emerges as the one most equipped to be the primary provider. This ability to provide grows out of the fact that in America on a national average, African American women, next to white men, are the largest wages earners. Black men nationally are ranked below white women in their annual income.

This ranking of black men at the bottom of the list on an annual basis is a reflection of a number of things such as racism and discrimination. However, in the context of this focus on parenting, the primary cause of the low annual income of black men is their inadequate education. In the black community it is the female that is pushed ahead in education by their family and society, whereas the males are most often left to make their own decisions about how much education they need.

In the 21st century the African American father must be empowered and equipped to function as the head of their family. This means acquiring the level of education that will enable him to function in job situations that are in the high income bracket. It means attacking racism and winning the right to hold any job in any company and forcing companies to be fair in hiring practices.

The role of African American man must be redefined so that they are able to model a more masculine male role in the home. The influence of mothers in the life of their sons, often with the absence of positive influence from the father, has produced men who know far more about being sons than they know about being men. This sonship tends to show up in men as strong tendencies for the domestic side of family life and little propensity for the aggressive male side of family life. In other words, young men today often feel that their role is to provide half the family income and do half the household chores. From a biblical perspective, the husband/father is the primary provider.

The African American father of the 21st century will need the time to be involved in the lives of his children on a daily basis. This means being available and willing to take charge of the son or daughter in cases where discipline is a problem. Fathers must be strong disciplinarians, and strong models of integrity and success.

As we move towards the 21st century, the watch word for the African American father is "challenge." The 21st century African American father will face a multitude of challenges. At the top of the list is the challenge of acquiring a level of education that will adequately equip him to compete with white men and black women in the marketplace. Winning in the marketplace is key in becoming a parent who effectively fathers his children. The very essence of fatherhood as set forth in the scriptures means being able to provide, protect, and control the household as a good shepherd.

The second major challenge the African American father will face and must win is in the arena of that which is spiritual. The spiritual vacuum that has so vividly evidenced itself in the lives of black men in the decade of the nineties must be filled in the 21st century with a relationship with Jesus Christ. The 21st century African American father will need a more positive attitude towards the black church. It was the black church that contributed most significantly to the positive development of black men in the post-slave and post-reconstruction eras. Those contributions included psychological liberation, leadership development, intellectuality, the family, economics, and social networking.

As was the black male in the early part of the twentieth century in this country, so are black men today and are likely to be in the 21st century in need of psychological liberation from a negative lifestyle that is hopeless and oppressive. The black church is key to this liberation. Black male leadership in the community is essential in developing boys into men with a positive self-image. To this end, the black church must provide leadership opportunities for men in the church and encourage and support black male leadership in the social and political arena in the community.

The intellectual development of black men must again be a primary focus of the black church. This means moving beyond the treasured emotional aspect of the black church into the arena of intellectual development of theologians and other Christian leaders.

In his relationship with and involvement in the church the black male will experience a revival of male authority in his home. In the arena of economics and social networking, the black church provides unlimited opportunity for the African American male to succeed.

MOTHERHOOD IN THE 21ST CENTURY

The African American woman must reject the image that was portrayed in the movie *Waiting to Exhale*. They must refuse to emulate Stella and go off trying to get their groove back, as is portrayed in the book *Stella Got Her Groove Back*. For while she is waiting to exhale, her children will likely suffocate and though she might well find her groove, she will most certainly lose her children.

The African American woman is the most evident model of womanhood in America. She is educated, sophisticated, professional, and strong. Black women are often different in terms of their social class, yet regardless of their class, all black women share much common ground in the areas of beauty, strength, and virtues. The challenge the black woman will face in the 21st century is investing in the development of black men with the goal of developing a stronger father for their children.

As a lover of nature, I watch a number of documentaries on animals. I am always intrigued with animals like the elephant, lions and others during the breeding seasons. The female will most often choose to mate with the male who has demonstrated the strongest qualities of that particular species. I am suggesting that black women will need to exercise much discretion among the limited choices they have for a mate in the next century. She must dare to wait until there is a quality male available with whom she can marry and grow strong children.

Womanhood in the 21st century for the African-American female will likely mean being willing to judge the quality of a man by the content of his character and not just his profession. Thus the African American woman will be more inclined to date men who are in a different social class than they are. This is not a new attitude on the part of black women for historically black women have married men who were not in their social class.

The African American mother will need to evidence

less authority in the home in her relationship with her children. This means being willing to permit her children to hold their father at the same level of respect and esteem as they do her. Thus she must determine to speak well of the father even when she does not agree with him.

The African American woman must choose to invest less in herself and more in black men. This means being less willing to be a critic of black men and more willing to be a supporter. Sometimes she must elect to hold herself back in order to give opportunity to the black man. In this context black women must preserve the dignity of the legacy of the noble black woman in terms of her moral commitment and example before her children.

Whereas the watchword for the African American male is "Challenge," for the female it is "Change." This change involves putting aside some of the different hats the African American female has worn for years.

The African American female of the nineties could boast and rightfully so, of being able to bring home the bacon, put it in a pan and still have the time and energy to take care of her man. Perhaps the best label for the black women today is "superwoman." The 21st century will likely demand less of black women and more of black men. This reduction in expectation and performance will be in the areas of income, parenting, and leadership in the church and community.

CHILDHOOD IN THE 21ST CENTURY

As I think of the Civil Rights Movement, beginning in the late fifties and continuing through the seventies, I remember the riots, the solders, the police, the violent dogs, and water hoses. What I most often fail to remember are the children, youth, and young adults who were so extensively involved in that movement.

In Little Rock at Central High School, one can easily see the mob of angry white people, the shouting mob of white students, the police and the military. However, if one looks closely they will see that in the midst of that mob was a small group of black children who put their young lives on the line to change a system. The same was true in New Orleans and other places where schools were being integrated.

The sit-ins at the lunch counters in the south were led by young black men and women. Some of them even gave their lives to change a system of legalized segregation that needed to be changed. These young people demonstrated unusual courage. They faced mobs, went to class day after day, absorbed the verbal and physical abuse from white students and teachers, and still passed their courses. This was extraordinary behavior.

The African American child in the 21st century must possess the courage to face opposition that will persist in social, political, educational and economic areas. The parents of the fifties, sixties and seventies grew children who were tough, courageous and smart. These children were raised to survive in the most difficult of circumstances. They could both give and take a punch when necessary. They did not expect to get anything for nothing. They knew how to work hard for what they wanted. Parenting in the 21st century will demand a return to that kind of parenting in which children are developed with tough skin, soft hearts, and strong heads. Children will be needed who are able to compete and survive in the world community. Children will be needed who refuse to accept handouts from the government, but choosing rather to fight and even destroy the system rather than be excluded from it because of their race.

In the 21st century African American boys will of necessity use their athletic skill to further the educational opportunities for their race. Some who go to college will need to major in the legal profession, economics, and political science with a view to creating a new judicial system that is less inclined to apply justice unequally.

The children of the 21st century must have a sense of nationalism that is strong but inclusive. It must be strong enough to foster strong self-image and self-esteem yet not of the kind that views others with disdain and hostility.

Finally, the children of the 21st century must become trained teachers and religious leaders. They must develop into the kind of adults who have the ability to lead in their own community. They must choose to value their achievements based on what they contribute to their own community and thereby to the world as a whole. They cannot afford to value only those abilities they have that have been labeled as valuable by the larger community.

Conclusion

There is a major deficit in the spiritual environment of the black community. This deficit is primarily a post-Civil Rights occurrence where the African American church lost the balance it had between the sacred and the secular. In the post Civil Rights era the black church tilted out of balance in favor of the secular, political, and the social. At the same time, African American men began to lose ground in the areas of education and employment combined with a turning away from the church.

The price of this shift in focus is evident in the loss of influence the black church has experienced over the past two decades in the lives of black men and the decline in the success of black children. Today there is a growing number of unchurched black men who have little sense of identity and purpose in their lives. This loss of leadership in the family and in the church is a primary contributing factor in the fractured structure of the black family.

In addition, the African American church has, in effect, abandoned the inner city urban communities to non-Christian religions and cults, the most prominent of these being the Nation of Islam. Inherent in this shift of the African American church away from the inner cities is an overt abandonment of the poor.

The Muslim faith has inherited those blacks who were historically the constituents of the black church. Those include the working poor, the welfare recipients, and the homeless. Those abandoned by the black church include the imprisoned who are largely male. These people have thousands of children. They comprise a very large portion of that group of people who are African American parents. The mega African American church whose membership is largely middle class along with the working class churches must pool their resources and return to the urban communities across this country and become involved in the ministry of rebuilding the African American families.

For many black leaders, the solution to the instability in the structure of the black family rests in new government policies such as affirmative action, welfare with work, and childcare. For others, the solution lies in black nationalism where some hold to teachings about Jesus Christ that are nothing less than paganism. The Million Man March on Washington, DC, showed that black men are in search of spiritual direction. There is a vacuum in their hearts from every level of the socioeconomic ladder. The black church must respond with the gospel .

It is not profitable for black preachers to send confusing signals to African Americans about the distinction between the message of Islam and Christianity. The need of black men today includes much more than a level of rehabilitation that turns them into effective paper boys on the corner. Black men need the gospel of Jesus Christ and they need to see the results of that gospel in the lives of Christian men at both the leadership level and the lay level in the home, church, and community.

Building and restoring the structure of the black family must begin with men at the level of the heart with the gospel of Jesus Christ. These men must be challenged to become strong family men by the models of Christian leaders. That is to say that mere words alone from church pulpits by strong orators are not sufficient for this task.

From Luke 5:10b comes a closing exhortation: After having been exposed to the sovereign power and holiness of God in his fishing boat and after having caught far more fish than they ever thought possible, Peter and the others are called to abandon their fishing profession and become fishers of men as full time disciples of Jesus. "From now on," said Jesus, "you will be catching men." He is calling these men to follow Him and He gives them a new agenda. The agenda is to catch men for the kingdom of God.

Since we are not children of a lesser god we must conclude that we too are to be fishers of men. To catch men, we must go where men are and we must preach Christ crucified and salvation by faith in the crucified and risen Christ—plus nothing. This is the way to restore the structure of the African American family and grow whole healthy adults in the 21st century.